TRUE HAPPINESS

Written & Compiled by L. M. Truqui
Revised by: Father James Fryar, FSSP
Edited by: Mrs. Laura Tellez, M.Ed., M.A.

HOLY FAMILY PRESS

First Printed in 2023

HOLY FAMILY PRESS

First Published in 2023

Revised by: Fr. James Fryar, FSSP

Edited by: Mrs. Laura Tellez, M.Ed., M.A.

ISBN: 979-8-218-96457-3

To the Most Blessed Trinity. Lord, please make me your humble servant.

To Mary, thank you for being the Star that guides us to the Safe Harbor!

For my beloved Salvador, Maria, and Jose. May the Lord grant you the grace to be always faithful seekers of the True Happiness.

To my parents Juan and Luchy, who have always loved me, supported me, and generously given their lives for their children.

With wholehearted gratitude to Fr. Fryar and Mrs. Laura Tellez, who so generously have taken time out of their extremely busy schedule to help with this book! I am deeply grateful!

INDEX

INTRODUCTION

In a world like ours, marked by so many opinions and differences, there is still something that unites us all: our deep desire to achieve the *true happiness*. In the midst of confusion, many times we find ourselves not knowing what to do or where to go; it is complicated to discover the incentives that help us to live joyfully and fulfilled! The result of this confusion and lack of motivation can be: divorce, solitude, depression, or suicide.

Even when the motivation and the answers seem to be far and unknown (on some occasions almost impossible to obtain) maybe they are closer to us than we think; in fact, they might just be at the reach of our hand! What are the "keys" to *the true happiness?* (those "keys" that help us to open the doors of clarity, which are necessary to understand where and how we must go in life) … My desire as I write this book is to show a path that will bring us directly to those keys—through clear, concrete, and simple ideas—so that after reading, the honest person may be able to find the truth, as he draws his own conclusions and judgements. The main source from which these thoughts and words have sprung, has been a sincere desire to help every person of good will to find the *true happiness*. If you are in search of joy and motivation, I pray that after reading this book, you may obtain the grace to start—or continue—unhesitatingly and joyfully, this *beautiful journey which is life*.

This book is intended for people who live, rejoice, love, suffer, hope … and who, sometimes, feel hopeless. If you have ever experienced any of these, this book is for you! I hope that you may enjoy it, and I pray that the Holy Spirit may instill in your heart those thoughts that might help you to grow and to reach your goals, especially the gift of a life lived in *peace* and *true happiness;* a happiness that does not pass or change because it is anchored in solid rock! Come Holy Ghost!

NOTE: To *facilitate* the reading, when I want to refer to both a masculine and feminine reader, most of the times I will use either "he" or "we." Thank you so much for your understanding and for staying with me through the reading of these pages. I so much appreciate you and value your time and attention!

CHAPTER I: Deeply Happy!

I received an email talking about the "happiest man in the world." He is a man of French origin, who—according to the research workers of the Affective Neuroscience Laboratory of the University of Wisconsin—by adopting a certain philosophy, has reached the highest levels of happiness to which a human being can ascend. According to the studies, this man achieved this "perfect happiness" through the total despoilment of everything: possessions, affections, and God. To discern the degree of truthfulness presented by these arguments, and to discover if total despoilment—as they present it—is the way to achieve the *true happiness*, let us consider the following thoughts:

A) *Detachment from the world and from material things*. In the 3rd century, a religious sect called the Manichaeans sustained that every material thing (including our body) is evil. But if God has said that everything that He has created is *very* good[1], who are we to affirm the contrary? "The world is not evil, because it has emerged from God's hands, because it is His creature, because when God looked at it, He saw that it was *good*."[2]

Disordinate attachment to material things *cannot* give us happiness because things (money, jewels, clothes, homes, cars, power, fame, etc…) might be in our possession today, but maybe tomorrow we will not have them. Certainly, the person who places *all* his hope in

---

[1] Genesis 1:31

[2] Saint Jose Maria Escriva - Homily pronounced at the University of Navarre, October 8, 1967.

those things will *surely* end up disappointed, depressed, and empty!

Nevertheless, God has bestowed upon us marvelous gifts through His creation, accompanied by the capacity to enjoy them. The Lord wants us to appreciate and enjoy everything that is good, beautiful, true, and legitimate. He knows that, through this delight, a sincere soul will be elevated to Him, the Creator and beginning of *every* good thing.

> *It is for this reason that I say that our times need to return to all matter—and to the situations which seem most vulgar—their noble and original sense; to put them at the service of the Kingdom of God, to elevate them to the spiritual realm, thus making of them a means and occasion of our continuous encounter with Jesus Christ.*[3]

Ordinarily, God does not ask us to be detached from everything. God asks us to *sanctify* our possessions by using them for His glory, for the good of others, and for our benefit. *Possessing* is a *blessing*, through which we are called to *share* with those who are less fortunate. *Not possessing* can also be transformed into a blessing ... How? By sharing our poverty with *Jesus*, who coming into the world <u>*chose*</u> poverty for Himself as a lifestyle. "The Birth of Jesus at Bethlehem reveals to us that God chose poverty for himself in coming among us ... *God chose this poverty....*" [4]

---

[3] Saint Jose Maria Escriva - Homily pronounced at the University of Navarre, October 8, 1967.

[4] Homily of Pope Benedict XVI during the Mass of the Solemnity of Mary Mother of God, Journey for peace in the world - Thursday, January 1st., 2009.

The true Christian understands that we cannot live in peace if we are embittered by ambition or envy before the material goods, possessions, and/or blessings of our neighbor. We must never allow ourselves to live in such spiritual agony … Not even when we are deprived of everything! The true Christian unites his desires and needs to Jesus'. "For you are well acquainted with the favor shown you by our Lord Jesus Christ: how for your sake He made himself poor though He was rich, so that you might become rich by His poverty" [5]. *Spiritual* poverty, manifested in *voluntary detachment out of love*, may be difficult at the beginning; but once it has been accepted and embraced, it brings great fulfilment, because "it is better to *need little* than to have much." [6] A true Christian *does not despise* material things … He sees them as they truly are—good, beautiful, and useful—but he keeps always in mind that they are just that, *things*. They are neither God, nor the end or goal of our life.

The first and most important motivation to be, live, think, act, and speak positively must spring from *within* and not from exterior circumstances. A life dependent on material things and on other people, is neither wise nor prudent. A faithful follower of Jesus Christ *uses material things* and what the world has to offer with *humility, moderation, gratitude, and generosity*. A true Christian is not *enslaved* by his possessions; he uses them with *freedom*. If for some reason he loses them, he learns to live without them (without bitterness or despair), because a Christian has his eyes set on the grandeur of the

---

[5] 2 Corinthians 8:9

[6] Saint Augustine, Bishop of Hippo. Father of the Church. (350-430).

horizon, which is open to infinite possibilities! The true Christian knows that life offers each one of us countless experiences which are beautiful and valuable (if we are open to receiving them)—including the moments in which it seems that we are amidst a storm.

We are not what we possess. We are not what we produce. *We are unique because we are loved by God!*

> *I implore you to start by adopting a new way of thinking: value a person, including yourself, not for what that person has but for what he or she is: a unique achievement of God's creative love ... Strive to apply this 'philosophy of being rather than having' ... You must not forget that the obligation to lead a simple life and to be detached from material things is an important part of Christian living.*[7]

Simplicity of life allows us to be detached from material possessions—not because they are evil, but because we want to imitate our Lord and Master—and to live with the *true* freedom of the children of God. In this way, whether we possess (many goods, talents, gifts) or not, our heart remains free and joyful; because the *true happiness* is not found in possession—nor in despoilment of everything—but in the *union* of our will with the holiest, purest, and most loving Will of *God*.

---

[7] Pope Saint John Paul II - Homily pronounced to the Youth at Willemstad, No. 7 – May 13, 1990.

B) <u>*Detachment from affections*</u>. "If you do not want to suffer, do not love, but if you do not love why would you want to live?" [8] We all need to love and to be loved. In the same way that the heart brings blood to the body and keeps it alive, so *love* is the water that makes our being bloom. Life can only be beautiful when we love *constantly*, even when this love may carry great sacrifices. As Mother Teresa of Calcutta stated: "true love is not love until it *hurts*".

In fact, loving is so important that, according to Saint Peter, "love covers a multitude of sins." [9] Once Saint Augustine, "the great sinner," embraced Jesus Christ in the Truth—after having left Manicheism—he wrote:

> *... love, the only debt which, even when it has been paid, holds him who has paid it a debtor still. For it is given when it is paid, but it is owing even after it has been given, for there is no time at which it ceases to be due.*[10]

Yes, we must try to love *always*, because *God is love*, and He has created us in His image and likeness. We, too, are called to be love! The saints have understood this, and through their love they have been able to transform the world. Saint Thérèse of Lisieux is a marvelous example: she entered the convent when

---

[8] Saint Augustin, Bishop of Hippo.

[9] 1 Peter 4:8

[10] Saint Augustine. Letter 192.

she was only 15 years old. Thérèse never left, but from her enclosure she wrote: "In the heart of the Church, I will be love."[11] Even though the "Little Flower" was a cloistered nun, today she is a Doctor of the Church and patron saint of the missions, and her love continues spreading and transforming hearts without borders!

Most certainly, our affections cannot "chain us," *enslave* us. But God has given us a heart to love. And thus, *only* when we love will we find fulfillment, because love *magnifies* what is small and brings us close to the Heart of Jesus. "I can assure you, my children, that when a Christian lovingly performs the most insignificant daily actions, these overflow with the transcendency of God." [12] Love is the noblest and most beautiful of all feelings, because "true love begins when we do not seek anything in return." [13] *True* love delivers peace, serenity, and strength.

Is it truly possible for an empty heart, for a person "empty" of affections, to attain the *true happiness?* "As poor as a table without bread, the most exemplary life without love, results empty." [14] My friend, let us be honest: a person despoiled of love neither can be happy nor can make others happy! We have been called to love (wherever we are, whatever we do). *Unconditional love* gives *meaning* to the emptiest lives. Let us not fear loving. Let us not fear having a heart *FULL* of love, full of *true* love (not of "caricatures" of love). Let us allow our love to overflow on all those around us, without seeking the recompense

---

[11] Saint Thérèse of Lisieux – Doctor of the Church (1873-1897).

[12] Saint José María Escrivá - University of Navarre, October 8th, 1967.

[13] Saint Thérèse of Lisieux – Doctor of the Church (1873-1897).

[14] Saint Anthony of Padua – Priest and Doctor of the Church (1195-1231).

on earth ... There is a much better and a greater reward awaiting us in Heaven!

C) Detachment from God. According to the email about "the happiest man in the world," *true happiness* resides in living totally free from any pressing situation, stress, or worry; it affirms that total despoilment of everything, including despoilment from God, can help us to achieve it. However, as Saint Augustine said, "You have made us for yourself, O Lord, and our hearts are *restless* until they rest in You." [15] God made us for Himself. Only in Him will we find our fulfillment and the *true happiness,* which is far greater than a smile or a life free of stress or grief! This is also clearly reflected in the lives of the saints. On many occasions they had to suffer great sorrows, hardships, pains, and even martyrdom. But all their sufferings were offered *voluntarily and out of true love.* Boundless hope shone in their souls, because they were centered in a far higher goal than themselves and their own satisfaction.

> *Five times I have received at the hands of the Jews the forty lashes less one. Three times I have been beaten with rods; once I was stoned. Three times I have been shipwrecked; a night and a day I have been adrift at sea; on frequent journeys, in danger from rivers, danger from robbers, danger from my own people, danger from Gentiles, danger in the city, danger in the wilderness, danger at sea, danger from false brethren; In toil and*

[15] Saint Augustine, Bishop of Hippo. Confessions I,1,1.

> *hardship, through many a sleepless night, in hunger and thirst, often without food, in cold and exposure. And, apart from other things, there is the daily pressure upon me of my anxiety for all the churches.*[16]

Saint Paul had to endure so many sufferings! Nevertheless, he was deeply happy, because his heart—far from being despoiled from God—was *firmly adhered* to Him. It was precisely in the Lord he loved, and in His grace—which he trusted—that Saint Paul found the strength to overcome *all* his trials and tribulations!

True despoilment of everything and true silence, far from separating us from God and each other, bring us closer to them. "The fruit of silence is prayer. The fruit of prayer is faith. The fruit of faith is love. The fruit of love is service. The fruit of service is peace" [17].

Considering all the above, it might be convenient to ask ourselves the following questions: Can a philosophical current (intellectual, economic, or social) which requires us to be despoiled from everything, make us truly joyful? Or rather—if led by these philosophies—are we not in real and grave danger of falling in deep spiritual emptiness and depression? Can we agree in the fact that *true happiness* cannot be found in despoilment of everything (with the only aim of arriving at nothingness—to be then absorbed into a different being)? May we unite our reason

---

16 2 Corinthians 11:24-28

17 Saint Mother Teresa of Calcutta.

and our hearts to recognize together that *the true happiness* is not found in despoilment of everything, but in *LOVE detached* from everything. This detached love is transformed into a marvelous—greater, and more generous—love. A type of love which fills and delights the soul of the person who gives away this transformed and humble "agape." [18] And also, this truthful love fills with joy and peace those who are open to receiving this gift with simplicity.

Finally, a word to my friends—who after reading much—have come to the conclusion that God does not exist: Why search in books what we can find by simply opening our eyes? Why do the planets have the right distance so that they do not crash against each other? Why does the Earth have the perfect conditions to be inhabited? Is there ever the same dawn or sunset? Are the mountains not majestic and the flowers not beautiful? Isn't our body made of hundreds of different cells which have life in themselves? Doesn't our body have organs which form systems that are necessary for it to work properly? Could the universe in all its grandeur and the amazing human being have been truly created by chance (by a mere explosion—emerging from nothing)? Aren't we, and *all* of creation, the work of a *very* Great and Powerful, a *very* Intelligent and Creative Person—who is *above* all, in every sense of the word?

On the other hand, if you have concluded that religion is useless and that there is no life after this one … Is there any sense to our sufferings—and to life itself? I hope that you may find an answer to these questions in the following pages!

---

[18] Greek word which refers to unconditional love. The highest form of love.

CHAPTER II: The Greatest Love

"This I command you: that you love one another." [19] If we really wish to find *true happiness* in our lives, it is essential to understand the *true* meaning of love. It is very easy to confuse love and feelings, or "chemistry" (as it is known nowadays). But *real* life demonstrates that love is far greater than feelings and physical attraction! *True* love implies *sacrifice, total surrender.* It is that attitude of "giving until it hurts," to which Mother Teresa refers: a willingness to sacrifice ourselves for the beloved, leaving ourselves behind, with the sole desire to make the person we love happy. "To love until it hurts" means doing everything possible just to bring peace into the beloved's life. At times this will entail depriving ourselves of what we like; to accept moments of solitude; to work "overtime." Other times it will mean enduring the hardships, the stresses, the difficulties. Many days it will mean to serve with joy even when our bodies are really tired. To love until it hurts can also mean to continue walking when we feel that we haven't gotten any strength left to do it. "To love until it hurts" means especially to keep our eyes fixed on Jesus. He—though weak and frail by fasting, the flogging, and the pain of His torn flesh—carried His cross to Calvary and died on it *for our salvation.*

"No one has a greater love than this, to lay down one's life for one's friends." [20] The greatest love is the one that makes *most sacrifices* for the beloved. The person who sacrifices most is the one who achieves the greatest degree of sanctification! This is the

---

[19] John 15:17

[20] John 15:13.

double beauty of love: on one hand, the person who loves makes others happy; on the other, he approaches the most perfect joy (which is union with The Love Incarnate, Our Lord Jesus Christ). Indeed, the person who loves most is the one who will reach the greatest degree of happiness in this life and in the next. When seen from this perspective, *true happiness* is not "...being understood, but understanding; being consoled, but consoling; being loved, but loving..." [21] These are Francis of Assisi's teachings. This beloved Saint through constant love, humility, and surrender resembled Christ so much that he obtained the grace of Jesus' five wounds in his own body. What are some of the qualities of *truthful* love?

A) *Love is service*. There cannot be any service without love, because then it becomes "servitude," *slavery*. The person who loves understands that *serving is loving*. Saint Peter, after receiving the Holy Spirit at Pentecost, blatantly proclaimed that Jesus "went about doing good." [22] To prove it, it is enough to open the Gospels and to contemplate Jesus throughout His public life. In the sixth chapter of Saint Mark [23] we find a good example of this love, transformed into service: Jesus and His disciples were so busy serving and helping people, that they didn't have time to

---

21 Prayer of Saint Francis of Assisi: "Lord, make me an instrument of your peace. Where there is hatred let me bring your love; where there is offense, let me bring your pardon; where there is discord, let me bring your unity; where there is doubt, faith; where there is error, truth; where there is despair, hope; where there is sadness, joy; where there is darkness, may I bring light. Oh, Master, grant that I may not seek to be understood, but to understand; to be consoled, but to console; to be loved, but to love. Because it is in giving that we receive, forgiving that we may be forgiven and dying that we are risen to eternal life".

22 Acts 10:38

23 Mark 6:30

eat. They went away in a boat and, as they landed, crowds were already waiting for them ... What was Jesus' reaction before them? Did He look at the people and, kindly, tell them, "I was with you all day, now I am tired and hungry, please go home and I'll see you tomorrow"? No! *Full of compassion*, after teaching them "many things," he fed five thousand men (plus their wives and children)! "This is the strength of love when it is perfect, that we forget our contentment, in order to content the beloved"[24].

B) *Love is forgiveness.* There is a well-known phrase from the novel *Love Story* by Erich Segal that says, "Love means never having to say you're sorry." However, according to Sacred Scripture, "the just man falls seven times." [25] The number seven means *infinity.* We must be conscientious of the fact that due to our fallen nature—many times without meaning to—we will offend and will be offended. Therefore, if we want to reach the *true happiness,* it is crucial to say, "I'm sorry" and to pray unceasingly for those whom we have offended—asking the Lord to heal what we have broken and are unable to restore—because *He* can.

Equally important is to be willing to accept, charitably and without complaints, the apologies offered to us (as hard as this might be—particularly when we have been badly hurt). Saint Augustine said, "If you are suffering from a bad man's injustice, forgive him, lest there be two bad men." Whoever forgives, especially the most hurtful offenses, *expands* his heart and becomes more *Christ-like*.

---

[24] Saint Teresa of Avila. Mystic and Doctor of the Church. (1515-1582)

[25] Proverbs 24:16

In the third century Tertullian said: "¿Do you want to be happy for an instant? Avenge! Do you want to be happy forever? FORGIVE!" Let us seek the *true happiness*, the one that lasts forever and ever. Let us forgive generously as God has forgiven us! When Saint Peter asked Jesus how many times he should forgive his brethren, the answer was clear, "Not seven, but seventy times seven." [26] Whenever we are requested forgiveness by a person who is *sincerely* repentant for having offended us, we *must* forgive! "For if you forgive men their trespasses, your heavenly Father also will forgive you; but if you do not forgive men their trespasses, neither will your Father forgive your trespasses." [27] Therefore, the *condition* to be forgiven, is *to forgive*; and to do it with the same generosity with which God gives us His generous and merciful love *every* day. We must forgive *everyone* (not only those who are just and good, but also, those who are evil and unjust). Seneca wrote in a letter to Saint Paul "Whomever hates the wrongdoers, hates everyone." In a heart full of love, there is no place for hatred! The person who loves *forgives*. This "forgiving from our heart"[28] frees and elevates our soul and prepares it to attain full happiness. Forgiving with humility and magnanimity, without any grudges, without humiliating the person who asks for forgiveness, is true, lasting, and restoring forgiveness.

The most sublime and humble love, manifested in forgiveness is this: "God shows His love for us in that while

---

[26] Matthew 18:21-22

[27] Matthew 6:14-15

[28] Truqui, Cesar. *Secretos para Perdonar de Corazón*, Editorial el Arca, S.A. de C.V., México, D.F., 2008.

we were yet sinners Christ died for us." [29] God has loved us in eternity and in time. Before we committed our worst sins—which were already in His sight—His immense love embraced us; He embraces us still. Being able to understand the depth of our sins and their consequences is extremely difficult and painful. We get a closer and more accurate look at our indignity and misery. Our unworthiness weighs heavily on us. Ashamed, we can be tempted to run away from the Lord—who is so Good, Pure, and Gentle—and from people, in general. And yet, we must remember that God knows our sins, and that in spite of that, He loves us still. He keeps trusting that we will change and become His *faithful* servants. Judas did not have this confidence in the Lord's love and forgiveness, nor in the beautiful mission that awaited him—and after betraying Jesus—he committed suicide. On the other hand, Saint Peter also betrayed the Lord; but he humbly recognized his sin, repented, and stayed close to Our Lady. Tradition tells us that Peter cried so much for having denied His Lord and Friend—who had loved him, taught him, fed him, and forgiven him countless times—that the tears formed a dent across his face. Because of his *sincere repentance* and resolution to make *amends* for his betrayal, Peter fulfilled his mission of being the "rock" on which Jesus' Church has been built.

Having knowledge of our sins is a great blessing if we humbly ask for forgiveness and try to repair the harm we have done, by sincerely loving and serving the Lord and others! God is waiting for us; He wants to help us become *new creatures*, who are in this world to love and to do good. "… Her sins, which are many, are

---

[29] Romans 5:8

forgiven, for she loved much." [30] It is true, our sins are *many* and we are *not* worthy, but the Lord forgives us and loves us with an infinite love! We need to approach God in His sacraments, especially in *confession* and in the most Holy *Eucharist*. Without him we remain in our nothingness and can fall into the deepest depression.

When we go to Mass, let us attentively hear—not only with our ears, but especially with our hearts—"Behold the Lamb of God, behold Him Who *takes away the sins* of the world" and let those words penetrate deep into our soul. Our sins are *NOT* bigger than Jesus' merits, love, and Mercy! We must have full *certitude* that Our Lord's death on the Cross has paid the ransom due so that we could be freed from our sins. This is how God forgives: totally and generously, to the point of giving His life, so that we can be saved and become holy in His sight—even when we have gravely sinned against Him and against others—as long as we are *sincerely* sorry, have an honest resolution to drastically *change* our life, and a humble desire to live only for His glory and for the well-being of His people, of *all* people. When we respond, "Lord I am *not* worthy that You should enter under my roof, but only say the word and my soul shall be *healed,*" we must remember that we are definitely *not* worthy, and so, we should draw close to Our Lady—like Saint Peter—and ask Her to pray on our behalf and to help us come to the Lord with a humble heart, begging that He heal our brokenness with His grace. " …A broken and contrite heart, O God, you will

[30] Luke 7:47

not despise."[31] God *can* heal and renew us if we humbly seek for Him and for His grace.

> *Come now, let us reason together, says the Lord: though your sins are like scarlet, they shall be as white as snow; though they are red like crimson, they shall become like wool. If you are willing and obedient, you shall eat the good of the land; but if you refuse and rebel, you shall be devoured by the sword ...*[32]

May the Holy Ghost pour into our souls the humility we need to repent, to stay close to our Good God, to help us love, and to allow ourselves to be loved—first by God, then by others.

Let us reflect on these thoughts constantly and let us ask for the grace of forgiveness frequently. If we keep in mind how much we have offended God and others, and His sweet and infinite forgiveness towards us *always*, accompanied by a new opportunity to start anew, when the moment arises, forgiveness will spring from a humble heart who knows his misery and the Trinity's bountiful love. We will be better able to forgive as a payment that we owe to the Good Lord.

C) <u>*Love means correction*</u>. Honestly, I have met only a handful of people who have the courage to correct and a few others who are grateful for correction. In the book of Genesis, we hear Cain

---

[31] Psalm 51:17

[32] Isaiah 1:18-20

saying, "Am I my brother's keeper?"[33] It seems as if today's love were inspired on that example: If your child makes a mistake, let him do it, sooner or later he will learn the lesson! If your friend errs, do not tell him, you don't want him to feel offended! If a neighbor, or someone you know does something incorrect, let it go, it is not your problem! But Saint Augustine teaches us that "evil is then rendered for evil, when one who ought to be rebuked is not rebuked, but by a wicked dissimulation, is neglected" [34].

In the book of Proverbs, Sacred Scripture shows us that "The Lord reproves him whom He loves, as a father the son in whom he delights." [35] If we love, we have to be very kind, good, tender, and patient: "The righteous one shall amend me in mercy" [36]; but also, we must be very firm and sincere. "It is better with severity to love, than with gentleness to deceive." [37] True love seeks what is good, and there is no greater good than the *eternal salvation* of the person we love. If his eternal salvation is in danger, we must tell him even when we feel we are "dying"—and even if the person we must correct feels that he is "dying" too.

Parents should *not* fear correcting our children, especially when they are young. This is the *best* time to do it! If our kids obey since they are little, they will understand the importance of obedience. They will know that there is always an authority above them. They will be successful in their enterprises, because having obeyed, they will know how to command!

---

33 Genesis 4:9

34 Saint Augustine. *On Rebuke and Grace*, 49 - Conclusion.

35 Proverbs 3:12

36 Saint Augustine, Bishop of Hippo. Commentary on Psalm 141,7.

37 Saint Augustine, Bishop of Hippo (Letter 93, Chapter 2,4).

> *Love and do what you will. If you keep silent, you will keep silent by love; if you make your voice heard, you will make it heard by love; if you correct, you will correct by love; if you pardon, you will pardon by love; if love is rooted in you, NOTHING BUT LOVE WILL BE YOUR FRUITS.* [38]

We must correct with love, out of love, and in The *Love*. Let us pray before giving a correction, so that it may be enlightened and blessed by the Holy Ghost.

Jesus teaches us: "If your brother sins against you, go and tell him his fault, between you and him alone. If he listens to you, you have gained your brother." [39] For this reason, Holy Mother Church has taught us that correcting the person who errs is a Work of *Mercy*. Let us see correction as it really is: a great act of love. May the Lord help us to be wise, courageous, and humble when we must correct! This loving correction is *not* going about the world judging the actions of others (constantly seeking for mistakes to "free" people from their error). Nobody could live with someone like this! Correction is intended especially to the members of our family and to our closest and dearest friends—those with whom we have ties of love and who have been placed in our life, so that we may offer mutual help to follow the path of goodness and truth, which leads to eternal life.

---

[38] Saint Augustine. Homily for Saturday in the Easter Octave – year 407.

[39] Matthew 18:15

Saint Paul, the great apostle who loved Christ, in his first letter to the Corinthians, magnificently summarized the true meaning of love. This fragment is so well known that maybe we already know it by heart; however, it might be useful to humbly consider if we truly put it into practice:

> *Love is patient, love is kind. It is not jealous, (love) is not pompous, it is not inflated, it is not rude, it does not seek its own interests, it is not quick-tempered, it does not brood over injury, it does not rejoice over wrongdoing but rejoices with the truth. It bears all things, believes all things, hopes all things, endures all things.*[40]

Let us ask the Lord for the grace to give abundant fruit, through a life lived in love. Only if we live loving (through sacrifice, total surrender, service, and forgiveness), if we live in *The Love*: Jesus Christ, the Incarnate Love—who became Man to show us how to love the Father and our neighbor—we will be truly happy.

Lastly: we need to remember that our love, sacrifice, surrender, service, and forgiveness are a pale reflection of the True Love. As Saint John said it, "In this is love, not that we loved God but that He loved us, and sent His Son to be the expiation for our sins." [41] The infinite, immense, and gratuitous love of God is the greatest, the most generous, the sweetest and purest. It is the most

---

40 1 Corinthians 13:4-7

41 1 John 4:10

selfless, patient, merciful, and the most perfect love of *all.* The person who receives love knows how to love. *Everyone*, without exception, is *abundantly loved by God.* Let us recognize this overabundance of God's love in our daily lives and ask for the grace to be able to share it (with the same generosity with which it has been given to us)!

CHAPTER III: The Lord's Admonishment

In the last chapter we recalled the fact that real correction, the one which *elevates and sanctifies*, is an act of *mercy*, born from a deep and sincere desire to *help* those we love. Nobody can ever love us more than *God*; for this reason, "the Lord's admonishment" or the "way of perfection," is the only path that leads us to the *true happiness*. We know admonishment is not easy, but seen as a path to happiness, it becomes beautiful and worth walking!

> *Let us rid ourselves of every burden and sin that clings to us and persevere in running the race that lies before us, while keeping our eyes fixed on Jesus ... for the sake of the joy that lay before Him, He endured the cross ... Consider how He endured such opposition from sinners, in order that you may not grow weary and lose heart.*[42]

We *cannot*, we must not, dismay because to be truly righteous and happy, and to achieve the virtues that will help us to go to Heaven, it is necessary to be *purified*. The Lord fulfills this purification "like gold in the refiner's fire."[43] To treat gold and rid it from every impurity—and thus, achieve its maximum splendor and value—the nuggets must be melted down at extremely high temperatures. This process must be repeated several times, until

42 Hebrews 12:1-3

43 Malachi 3:2-3

the image of the refiner is reflected on the surface of the melted gold; then and only then, it is ready. Likewise, God must purify us *repeatedly*, until He is able to recognize *His* image in us![44] We must be courageous when facing sufferings and trials if we wish to be a "mirror" of the Lord. We must generously accept being purified *several* times, trusting that the "Refiner" knows what He is doing in our souls. If we trust God, at the end of the process, we will be able to bring His Presence and message to those we encounter in our daily lives.

In our tribulations and moments of difficulty, let us remember to maintain our gaze fixed on the Lord. He can *always* help us! Let us not dismay, lose heart, nor feel disappointed. Since God is our Creator, He knows us perfectly well—even better than we know ourselves. He is omniscient (infinitely wise), and therefore, He understands with absolute clarity what is best for us. In our setbacks and trials let us find *rest*, because the Lord *takes care of us* with immense love, and He will grant us what is best for the salvation of our soul. God loves us; God listens to us. Let us remember what Saint Teresa of Avila said, "God writes straight with crooked lines." The Most Blessed Trinity can transform evil into good if we remain close to Him and do not lose hope—not even in the moments of darkness when we are tempted to despair. At the proper time, God will respond [45], transforming the night into day. Saint Micaela of the Blessed Sacrament said: "The saints were not born saints; they achieved holiness after a long succession of

---

44 Ecclesiastes 2:1-6

45 Luke 18:7-8

self-denying actions." [46] We cannot enter Heaven through the "wide door." [47] We must enter through the "narrow door"—allowing the King to correct us, purify us, and guide us—until our wedding garment [48] is ready, so we may come in and enjoy the eternal Banquet with Him.

Inspired in Saint Augustine's words: "Grant what you command and command what you Will" another phrase was born: "God does not command impossible things, but when He commands what He commands, He invites you to *do* whatever you can, and to *ask* for what you can't … and He helps you so that you can." There is nothing impossible when we are on God's side (even when everything seems impossible, painful, dark, and complicated). Just as when we look directly at the sun and become blinded, it may happen that, when God is extremely *near* to us, it may seem the darkest moment of our life! There can be times in which we see and feel Him not … Yet, undeniably, the Lord is *always* at our side. God is faithful, and when a person accepts the mission entrusted to him by the Lord, the Blessed Trinity sends abundant graces to sustain him in his efforts. Can there be a more beautiful ideal than this: of becoming "the hands, feet, eyes, and mouth" of the Lord? Can there be a more noble goal than to aid and console the afflicted, to give light to the spiritually blind, and to extend our hand to the fallen?

This is Charles de Foucault's prayer:

---

46 Saint Micaela of the Blessed Sacrament. Spanish Religious Sister (1809-1865).

47 Luke 13:24

48 Mateo 22,12

> *Father, I place myself into Your hands, do with me as You wish. Whatever it is, I thank You. I am ready for everything. I accept everything, as long as Your Will may be fulfilled in me and in all of Your creatures. I do not desire anything else, Father. I entrust my soul to You. I give it to You with all my love, because I love You and I need to give myself to You: to place myself in Your hands without measure, with an infinite trust, because You are my Father.*

And Pope Benedict XVI said:

> *The Lord wishes to make each one of us a disciple who lives in personal friendship with Him. To achieve this, it is not enough to follow Him and to listen to Him outwardly: it is also necessary to live with Him and like Him. This is only possible in the context of a relationship of deep familiarity, imbued with the warmth of total trust. This is what happens between friends; for this reason, Jesus said one day: '...No longer do I call you servants, for the servant does not know what his master is doing; but I have called you friends, for all that I have heard from my Father I have made known to you.'*[49]

[49] General Audience, July 5, 2006.

Jesus, our Great Friend, has suffered. We must suffer *with Him*, until His image is reflected in us. We must pass through this purification with great *patience* and *humility*, and with full confidence, begging for the Lord's aid at every moment. We will *only* be able to conquer the battles of life if we count on *His* grace. "Without Me you can do nothing"[50].

In an article published in *THE TOWER,* dated February 17th, 2020, Renée Rasmussen summarized Immaculee Ilibagiza's conference on February 13th, 2020 at the Catholic University of Washington. On this occasion she explained how, after surviving the killing of hundreds of people of the Tutsi Tribe in Ruanda—including her *whole* family (parents, siblings, uncles, aunts, and cousins)—she heard the voice of the Lord, telling her: "If you choose love, if you choose goodness, I am with you." Immaculee listened and chose the path of love and goodness. Her cross *purified* her, and her humility has obtained for her the greatest reward: friendship with the Lord and becoming a mirror of His Mercy and forgiveness for all of us to see and understand.

> *To ascend to God, man must be purified: 'The way that leads human nature to Heaven is none other than detachment from the evils of this world.' Becoming like God means becoming righteous, holy, and good.* [51]

---

50 John 15:51

51 His Holiness Pope Benedict XVI. General Audience –Sept.5, 2007.

This goal of a *purified* soul is not easy, but it is pleasing to God, because Jesus told us: "Be perfect as your Heavenly Father is perfect" [52].

When the Sacred Heart of Jesus appeared to Saint Margaret Mary Alacoque, He told her: "If you want to love Me, trust in Me; If you want to love Me much, trust much; if you want to love Me without limits, trust without limits." If we want to love Jesus and to achieve the *true happiness,* we must allow God to purify us, keeping our sight fixed on Him, trusting *without limits* in His love and goodness. He is our Best Friend and our Good Father. He is the *most* interested in our eternal salvation. He has clearly proven it by suffering the painful and humiliating death on the Cross, only *for our* salvation!

[52] Matthew 5:48

CHAPTER IV: «By this Sign You Will Conquer»

Constantine's conversion was the immediate result of a vision which he had before The Battle of Milvian Bridge on October 28, 312. This vision occurred in two parts. The first one: as he was marching with his soldiers, they all saw the form of a cross in front of the Sun beside the words: *"In Hoc Signo vinces"* (by this Sign you will conquer, abbreviated IHS; letters that are also used when we refer to Jesus: *"Iesus Hominum Salvator,"* Jesus the Savior of mankind). The second vision was a dream, in which he was commanded to put a new symbol on his military standard; one that he would call the labarum or "chreston" (the representation of the monogram of Christ). And, surely enough, despite the fact that he was fighting against the Roman emperor and military expert, called Maxentius, with God's help —which is always more powerful than any enemy—Constantine emerged victorious!

The Cross of Christ obtained the victory for Constantine, and Christ's Cross is still obtaining victories for each one of us. Nonetheless, it seems as if we were still living in Saint Paul's times, when the Cross was regarded as a "stumbling block" and " foolishness." [53] It seems as if we consider the cross to be a "curse," and we desperately want to get rid of it.

How many of us are really willing to embrace our cross, and to deny ourselves to follow Jesus every day? [54] When faced with difficulty, do we turn our gaze to Him, who for love of us

---

[53] 1 Corinthians 1:23

[54] Matthew 16:24

died Crucified? In how many homes do we find a Crucifix on the wall, as a reminder of Jesus' loving sacrifice for our salvation? Do we find in the *Lord* the strength to keep going on and the answer to our most sorrowful questions and doubts? Saint Paul said, "But may I never boast except in the cross of our Lord Jesus Christ"[55] … Have we fully embraced Saint Paul's attitude towards life? There are some physical and/or spiritual sufferings that can *only* be healed by Christ's Cross: the greatest and deepest sorrows—those that are only known by God and us and which lay "hidden" in the deepest corner of our soul and being. The Cross is our *only* true healing balm. Why then, are we so fearful and persistent in our desire to get rid of it, when in fact, it is *sweet* and *healing* for our soul?

Our crosses may come into our life in many different ways and shapes—in the form of physical, emotional, or moral sufferings or as depression; sometimes they come from unknown reasons, but in other occasions, from well-known reasons: from unbalanced chemical levels in the brain; because of our personality; by worries (like seeing our children going astray through vice); by economic problems or hunger; as the consequence our own sins, wrong decisions, or mistakes. Or maybe they have befallen upon us involuntarily, without any fault of ours: by sickness (personal, or the sickness of those we love); by natural disasters; or by the free will of someone (by their distraction, ambition, selfishness, lust, pride, etc.) … Regardless of the cause, it is very important to seek the strength we need in the Lord, to take up our cross and follow Jesus with *confidence* and *humility*. He is at our side, He will *never* ask us for more than what we can bear, and

---

[55] Galatians 6:14

He will *never* leave us alone! These sufferings—which are our crosses—far from being impediments and a hindrance to our life and happiness, are rather "the sign by which we will *conquer*." They are our way to Heaven. As painful as they are, our sufferings—if carried with love, humility, and with a positive spirit—become gifts from God, opportunities to love and to grow in friendship with the Crucified.

> *Our life is a pilgrimage, and as such, it is full of difficulties. But our maturity is forged in hardships. No one knows himself except through trials; nor receives a crown, except after victory; nor becomes victorious except he fights; nor fights except he has enemies.* [56]

The Cross is the symbol of the *true* friends of Christ. Surely, during our life we will experience sufferings. We have two options: either taking up our cross and following Christ—firmly adhered to Him—and thus, finding the way to peace and holiness; or dumping our cross, rebelling against God, and becoming bitter and hopeless for the *rest* of our lives.

There is an apostolate in the United States which is called "Silent No More Awareness." Through this apostolate, women who have finished with the life of their child in the womb expose with full honesty the *huge* cross that their decision has brought into their life. Devastating havocs! They hope to repair the damage caused

---

[56] Saint Augustine, Bishop of Hippo. *Commentaries on the Psalms*, No. 60.

to their baby and to themselves by trying to share their terrible experiences with other people. Their desire is to help other women, so that by knowing the *truth*, they may not commit their same mistake. These courageous women share the experience of their deep sorrow, guilt, sleepless nights, eating disorders, infertility, troubled relationships, and the depression that they have experienced after the death of their child. Many of them have started speaking after long years of silence—when they finally opted for freedom—after finding peace in their faith, in the Crucified Jesus' embrace, and in the Lord's magnanimous forgiveness. These women's experiences have led me to seriously reflect on the great number of men and women who suffer from depression in the United States and in the whole world … Yes, willingly ending a pregnancy causes huge ravages in the mind, soul, and heart of the person who makes this *terrible* choice. It devastates lives, bodies, consciences, and personal relationships. Those mothers, fathers, and grandparents—who voluntarily go to a clinic with the desire to terminate forever the innocent life of the most precious and tiny member of their family—will never be the same!

If you are contemplating the termination of your pregnancy as an option, please listen to this cordial and humble invitation to reconsider your decision. I'll never meet you. Nevertheless, because you are a child of God, you are *very* important to me. My only desire is the best for your life. Consider how, in the same way that God created Eve from the side of Adam, God creates a new life from the union of a man and a woman, from the flesh and blood of the mother. There is a very intimate relationship between mother and child: that little babe is truly flesh of her flesh and blood of her blood. In a mysterious way, if the son rejoices, the mother rejoices; if he suffers, the mother suffers; if he dies, a part of her dies too! Remember that "something dies within the mother, when her child dies." After having voluntarily ended the life of a baby, the parents' life will be missing a *very* important part of themselves that will remain void *forever*!

Let us engrave in the deepest part of our soul the certainty that maternity and paternity are *extraordinary* gifts, a present from God. Children, according to the Catechism of the Catholic Church, are the "crown" of their parents.[57] Kids are marvelous, and if for some circumstance they become our "cross," they are an "easy and light" burden [58]; an opportunity to *grow* in a virtuous, humble, and sacrificial love. There are many couples who cannot have babies, and who are willing, hopeful, and who would joyfully adopt yours—if you believe that you are unable to provide for his needs. Please, do not deny your baby the opportunity of being born, of growing, of becoming someone "great" and beautiful. Allow him to become a gift for humanity! Will you be the mother of a new Pasteur, of another Padre Pio, of a new Mother Teresa of Calcutta? *You* are the only aid with which your baby counts on for food, health, and LIFE!

On the other hand, if you or someone you love has had the misfortune of making the wrong choice—and has terminated the life of her baby—I humbly invite you to grow closer to the

---

[57] Catechism of the Catholic Church - No. 1652.

[58] Matthew 11:30

Crucified Jesus. Talk to Him from the bottom of your soul, find in Him the reconciliation and the peace that you so much desire and that you so much need. Only in this friendship you will find *the true happiness*. Embrace Christ's Cross, "take up your cross" [59] and follow Him with full confidence, because He loves you *very* much! He is waiting for you. He has been waiting for you in the Sacrament of Confession for a *long* time. He wants to give you His embrace, forgiveness, understanding, and His grace to sustain you in your daily battles. Do not leave the Lord waiting any longer … do not delay any longer your encounter with *true* peace!

Remember Jesus' words throughout the Gospel, words frequently repeated also by Pope Saint John Paul II: "Do not be afraid!" Why be afraid of God who is *love*? How can we be afraid of the Person who loves us most—to the point of giving His life for us on the Cross (though we have constantly offended Him)? While Jesus was hanging on the Cross, He already knew everyone's story of failure and success, of sin and grace. While He was bleeding and dying for our sins, each one of us was present within His Heart. The thought of *you* and *me* gave Him the strength He needed to surrender His own life to the *extreme*; He already recognized us as His beloved. He already knew what every person would go through during his entire life: the thoughts, concerns, anxieties, and fears; the choices we would make, the sins we would embrace. And the Incarnate God did not draw back: He died—having been flogged, crowned with thorns, and excruciatingly pierced—because we are *ALL precious* in His sight!

---

[59] Luke 9:23

In the moments of trial, suffering and doubt (when we do not understand the reason for things to happen; when we do not know what to say or how to act)—if we wish to be true Christians—we must turn our eyes to *Jesus Crucified* and find in *Him* the answers that we seek. Jesus, from the Cross, gives us the greatest lesson: keeping silent, being patient, loving, and giving everything for those who mistreat us and hate us … We are called to love and to act like Jesus. *He* is our best Model! "In the midst of a world marked by brokenness and by lack of communion, the cross is a sign of reconciliation with God, with ourselves, with humanity and with the whole creation"[60].

We can find in Jesus' Cross a marvelous "balance," an unlimited strength, a joy far greater than the one acknowledged and given by the world; a joy that "no one will take away from us" [61] because our crosses make us *unique* and *very special!* The Lord is *always* with us, at our side (even when we cannot see Him, do not feel Him … or even when we do *not want* to see Him or to listen to Him!) God is *always* faithful and His love for us *never* changes. Let us remain at His side and never abandon Him. If we endure our trials *with* Him, we will *conquer!* Jesus told us: "In the world you have tribulation; but be of good cheer, I have overcome the world" [62] and God *never* lies! United to Him we will be victorious like Constantine—even against the greatest enemies!

Let us be grateful for Jesus' Cross. And for love of Him, let us embrace our own crosses, always keeping in mind that: "by this

---

60 Aciprensa – January 25, 2009.

61 John 16:22

62 John 16:33

sign *we will conquer*." The cross is not empty. On it we find Jesus Christ crucified for *love* of *us*. The world can revolve, turn around, and be placed upside down; people can love us or hate us; things may go well or wrong … If we are united to God—who loves us and understands us, who knows our intentions and limitations, who always forgives us and aids us—*everything* is and will be alright!

CHAPTER V: "Dressed" in Brown

In the following lines we will try to see the importance of "dressing up in brown" to achieve the *true happiness*. Ridiculous? Please continue reading! ... Why should we like dressing up in brown? This is a very simple question that may seem trivial, but which is truly important. Don't worry! I am not talking about exterior clothing, but about our interior attire. Why is it important to have a *soul* "dressed" in brown? The color brown is related to the virtue of *humility* because soil is brown, and we cannot stand on anything lower than the earth under our feet, in fact, the word humility comes from the Latin *humus*: earth, soil or ground. Also, because the color brown does not usually stand out among the crowds. What does this have to do with *the true happiness?* Much more than what we can imagine!

This chapter will be divided in two sections. The first one describes humility and its relationship to happiness. The second one suggests some forms in which we can put it into practice in our daily lives.

A) *Why does humility help us to achieve happiness?*

a. *Humility fills our soul with peace.* There is only one virtue in which Jesus places Himself as an example; it is humility. "Learn from *me,* for I am meek and humble of heart ..." [63] The Lord ends

[63] Matthew 11:28-30: "Come to me, all you who labor and are burdened, and I will give you rest. Take my yoke upon you and learn from me, for I am meek and humble of heart; and you will find rest for yourselves. For my yoke is easy, and my burden light".

up this phrase by explaining the reason for which we must live this beautiful virtue: "you will find *rest for your souls*." In the Gospels, Jesus shows us the key to obtaining this rare and so desired wealth which is peace. This "key" is *humility!* "By humility mankind finds grace before God and peace with his brethren." [64] How many of us can sincerely say that we live in peace? Peace in our souls and in society is so rare that we could call it "a treasure:" it is truly *precious* and *difficult* to find. Jesus said to His disciples, "Peace I leave with you; my peace I give to you." [65] Why then have we lost peace in our world, in our country, in our families, and in our souls? Could the answer be that we have forgotten—or maybe *despised*—the virtue of humility, which is so *essential* for our lives and our relationships? Could it be because our ears have become deaf to Jesus' soft and loving voice within us, and to His Gospel teachings? "The humble live in continuous peace, while in the hearts of the proud are envy and frequent anger." [66]

b. *God loves the humble.* We live in a world full of luxuries, comfort, and diverse occupations. With ease, we can forget that the *true happiness* (unchanging happiness) is rooted in friendship with God, because *God never changes*. We need to constantly remember Saint Teresa of Avila's words: "...God alone is

---

64 Blessed Gil of Assisi. Member of the first group of followers of Saint Francis of Assisi. (1190-1262).

65 John 14:27

66 Tomas de Kempis – *The Imitation of Christ*. First Book, Chapter VII.

unchanging… God alone suffices" [67]. The humble person lives in search of the *unchanging* God.

If we truly want to live in friendship with the Lord, we need to ask for the grace of *practicing* humility. It is a *condition* to know God well because the soul that is full of himself has no space available for anything or anyone else. Since it is *very difficult* to find love in the soul that is *self-obsessed*, God can *only* make His dwelling place in a *humble* soul. The Lord—who is Love—seeks for souls with whom He can identify: humble souls, full of love. When He finds them, He pours out His Spirit within them: "The Spirit of wisdom and understanding, the Spirit of counsel and might, the Spirit of knowledge and the fear of the Lord" [68].

The virtue of humility helps us to understand God's love for us. When a soul is aware of God's love for him, his life changes radically. May the Lord help us to seek and understand His love for us through a *humble and simple* life. "For thus says the High and lofty One who inhabits eternity, whose name is Holy: 'I dwell in the high and holy place, and also with him who is of a *contrite* and *humble spirit* …'" [69] The Sacred Heart is beating, enkindled in love for us. He awaits us to "revive our contrite hearts" through His ineffable tenderness. O Lord—who love us so much—help us to be emptied of ourselves so that we may be filled with your infinite love and find in *You* the *true* and *unchanging happiness*. Amen.

---

67 «Let nothing trouble you, let nothing scare you. All is fleeting. God alone is unchanging. Patience obtains everything. Who possesses God wants for nothing. God alone suffices!»

68 Isaiah 11:2

69 Isaiah 57:15

c. "*With humility the Earth is renewed... joy is enkindled and song is born...*" In his homily during the Christmas Mass of 2007, His Holiness Pope Benedict XVI (a humble Pope gifted with an extraordinary spiritual depth), said:

> *In the stable at Bethlehem, Heaven and Earth meet. Heaven has come down to Earth. For this reason, a light shines from the stable for all times; for this reason, joy is enkindled there; for this reason, song is born there... Heaven does not belong to the geography of space, but to the geography of the heart. And the heart of God, during the Holy Night, stooped down to the stable: the humility of God is Heaven, and if we approach this humility, then we touch Heaven. Then the Earth too is made new ... Let us touch God's humility, God's heart! Then His joy will touch us and will make the world more radiant.*[70]

Let us go out to the encounter of God's humble Heart, which is Heaven. Let us ask Him for the grace of a heart like His. If we are assisted by His *grace*, we will be able to build a *brighter* and more *joyful* world (for ourselves and for others). Aided by the virtue of humility we will see kindness and spiritual beauty in others, and the desire to treat them with love, generosity, and respect will increase in our hearts. How many humble, "great," and good souls do we find on our daily journey? Do we appreciate

---

[70] Homily of the Holy Father Benedict XVI – Christmas 2007.

them? Do we try to find the spiritual beauty which lays in the soul of every person? Do we really want to make of this a better world, "to renew the face of the Earth" and to live with joy? Maybe the Lord is inviting us to "dress up in brown" to achieve this most glorious victory!

d. *Humility helps us to get to Heaven.* A humble and trustful heart is like the heart of a little child. Who can be happier than a little kid? Jesus told His disciples, "Let the children come to me… for the kingdom of God belongs to such as these." [71] Humility provides the *true happiness*, because it is a *sure* road to eternal life … And a path to this humility is *unlimited* trust in Divine Kindness and Providence. The Most Blessed Trinity desires to live eternally surrounded by His beloved family. *Every* human being is God's family—a *cherished* child of God. God longs for each one of us to be with Him in Heaven, forever. A good father only desires the wellbeing of his children. If they understand their dad's love for them, they automatically believe in him—and trustful—they obey him. God loves *all* His children, but especially His "little" child: His *humble* and *obedient* child. This "little" soul, in his humility, is not embarrassed to openly manifest his own misery and God's greatness—in which he places all his trust. The Lord never lets down the humble soul, because even when things don't go his way, the humble person continues trusting in God's wisdom and love. This attitude fills God's Heart with joy and hope (and opens the gates of Heaven for the humble)!

---

[71] Mark 10:13-16

e. *Humility helps us to be free.* In Saint John's Gospel, Jesus told us. "You will know the truth, and the truth will make you free."[72] As a consequence of relativism, it would seem as if the truth were irrelevant; in this current of thought, each one appears to possess the absolute truth: "this is *my* truth" "this is what seems good and right *to me*" "what *I* say and do is correct; it is right, because it makes *me* happy." Nevertheless, when Jesus was brought before Pilate, He told him: "For this I was born, and for this I have come into the world, to bear witness to the truth." [73] This is the immense importance of The Truth: Jesus gave His life for it! With so much confusion prevailing in our days, we could be asking ourselves the same question as Pilate, "What is the truth?" [74] Jesus, our faithful friend, has already answered: "I am the way, *the truth* and the life."[75] Jesus Christ *is* The Truth. He is always with us, but He desires that we search for Him. Saint Augustine—in a letter to one of his disciples—tells us what is the *only* way through which we will find Christ: "I wish you to prepare for yourself no other way of seizing and holding the truth, than that which has been prepared by [God] … in that way the first part is humility; the second, humility; the third, humility." Therefore, to be free, we must know and live in the truth. And to reach the truth, we must be *humble!*

f. *Humility is essential to acquire every other virtue.* "Humility is the fundament of every other virtue. If a person lacks this attribute,

---

[72] John 8:32

[73] John 18:37

[74] John 18:38

[75] John 14:6

there cannot be any other virtue, but only as mere appearance" [76] ... and we cannot get to Heaven through appearances, but only with *proven virtue*, which is based on humility. Should we "dress up in brown"? Most definitely because we will only get to Heaven once we are attired for the eternal Banquet [77] with baptismal grace, cultivated and embellished by a sincere effort to live a virtuous life: a life which constantly strives to glorify God and to never offend Him voluntarily. A life which becomes resplendent by the virtue of humility through which the soul "diminishes", allowing God "to grow" [78], until the person is able to repeat with Saint Paul "It is no longer I who live, but Christ [the perfection of every virtue] who lives in me" [79].

B) Some ways in which we can put humility into practice. Each one knows which is his "stumbling block." We must firmly "attack" that specific defect which makes us fall more frequently on our way to perfection. The following are some ideas that might be helpful to achieve this ideal of a humble life:

a. *To seek always and in everything God's glory, and not our own.* The easiest—or most appealing way to our fallen nature—is doing things to be seen, praised, "applauded," commended, "admired." Sometimes we wish that people would "understand" how "intelligent" we are, and all the "good" things that we have

[76] Saint Augustine, Bishop of Hippo.

[77] Matthew 22:12

[78] John 3,30

[79] Galatians 2:20

accomplished. We want to make sure everyone knows how hard we have worked to achieve what we have and to be who we are. Nonetheless, the most meritorious and beautiful attitude—and the most helpful to grow in humility—is to make everything with only one intention: that GOD may be known, praised, loved, and glorified in the whole world—but also in our person, words, actions, writings, and even in our silence and in our nothingness.[80] In other words: to *disappear*, so that *God* may appear. Following the example of Saint John the Baptist, let us repeat, "He must increase, but I must decrease."[81] Most importantly, let us follow Jesus' example, who "emptied Himself, taking the form of a slave"[82].

Cardinal Saint John Henry Newman wrote a prayer which illustrates the depths of a soul who is truly humble and in love with God. This prayer became one of Mother Teresa of Calcutta's favorites, and it goes like this:

> *Dear Jesus, help me to spread your fragrance everywhere I go. Flood my soul with your Spirit and Life. Penetrate and possess my whole being so utterly that all my life may be only a radiance of Yours. Shine through me, and be so in me, that every soul I come in contact with, may feel Your presence in my soul. Let them look up, and see no longer me, but only Jesus! Stay with me, and then I*

---

80 Matthew 6:1-6.

81 John 3:30.

82 Philippians 2:5-8

> *shall begin to shine as You shine; so to shine as to be a light to others. The light, O Jesus will be all from You! None of it will be mine. It will be You, shinning on others through me. Let me thus praise You, in the way which You love best: by shining on those around me. Let me preach You without preaching; not by my words but by my example; by the catching force, the sympathetic influence of what I do, the evident fullness of the love my heart bears for You. Amen.*

b. *Not being presumptuous about what we are, nor about the things we possess.* Let us remember, "Who confers distinction upon you? What do you possess that you have not received? But if you have received it, why are you boasting as if you did not receive it?" [83]

The color of our eyes, skin, and hair; our height, IQ, and our family … Everything has been given to us as a gift! Wealth, corporations? Who has given us the health and intelligence that we need to make them prosper and to be successful? Absolutely everything has been given to us—and we preserve what we have—only by God's Will and generosity, because *all* good things come from the Lord! Whatever we possess and enjoy we owe solely to the Lord's Most Holy Will, infinite Mercy, generosity, and kindness! I hope that we do not need a proof of this fact, but if it were necessary, reading the book of Job in the Sacred Scripture, can be highly illustrative. To finish this section, let us use for our personal reflection Saint Augustine's phrase: "Pride is not

[83] 1 Corinthians 4:7

greatness, but swelling; and what is swollen seems big, but it is not healthy".

c. *Being happy with the things that we can achieve and with the things that we can own—and sharing always.* We must constantly toil to achieve and obtain what is good and noble. We need to make our best effort in all we do, and work with determination. We should strive to be better and move forward, because if we do not advance, we will go backward.

> *Never be satisfied with what you are, so that you may become what you are not. If you say 'enough,' you are lost. Advance always, do not stop on the way, do not go back, do not deviate. Whoever does not advance, goes backward. I prefer a lame man on the good road than a runner out of it.*[84]

However, there might be times in which we work and wear away to achieve an ideal, health, a job, a material or a spiritual good—and although we diligently strive for it—we still cannot obtain it. In those difficult times, we must find our *peace* in humility. And even amidst neediness and hardships, we should *share*—like the widow who donated very little to the offerings, but was praised by Jesus because she gave "her whole livelihood"[85]. With total sincerity, let us seek within our hearts to know and do

---

[84] Saint Augustine, Bishop of Hippo. Sermon 169,18.

[85] Luke 21:1-4

God's Will. In the measure of our possibilities, let us give the *best* of our goods and resources at the service of the Lord and of others. Above all, let us give the best of *ourselves*: our time and attention; our qualities, and our smile. "God loves a cheerful giver." [86] Don't we *all* appreciate a cheerful giver, too? A person who tends to be depressed, thinking about his miseries all the time; he who lets everyone know about his sorrows and difficulties—in order to manipulate and obtain compassion—very soon will be alone!

The humble heart will smile, even when he is not feeling "excellent," because he wants to make the life of others better; and by doing this, he makes his own life so much bearable! God "is never outdone in generosity". Nothing is concealed from the Lord. Each and every one of our efforts will be abundantly rewarded by Him!

d. *Obeying God and accepting humiliations and contempt.* Sometimes obeying God will not be easy. It will entail humiliation, being despised, and mocked by others. It may even entail asking forgiveness from the person who has offended us (when, for some reason, the person who has offended *us*, feels offended *by* us!) This is difficult. But the humble soul receives all these trials as coming from the loving hand of God; as opportunities for reparation for his own sins and offenses, which—this soul understands—have been the cause of Jesus' Cross. The humble person takes humiliations and contempt as opportunities to contribute in Jesus' redemptive mission (offering up his sufferings for the conversion of sinners

[86] 2 Corinthians 9:6-7

and the salvation of souls). The humble soul sees humiliations as being *fair* and *well-deserved.* He discovers that they can become a means for personal *sanctification* and an *opportunity* to get close to the Lord, who—doing good—received in return spitting, scorn, and mockery … How much more we, who are evil, should *lovingly accept* all our tribulations!

In four of the apparitions of the Blessed Virgin Mary at Lourdes, Saint Bernadette Soubirous received from "the Lady" the commandment: "Go to the spring, drink, and wash yourself in it." There was only one problem: in that place, there was only mud and filth because it was a pigsty! Yet, Bernadette, obeyed. Obviously, the people were scandalized; they mocked and laughed at her. They called her crazy ... A little while later, a miraculous spring appeared. This spring has been the cause of innumerable physical and spiritual miracles. Bernadette did not wish to receive praises; she had humbly obeyed, and God had worked *His* miracles. Sometimes God will require us to go through humiliations and "madness." In these moments—if we wish to grow in humility—we should remember that we must be willing to "do the ridiculous, so that God works the miraculous" in our soul and in the life of others.

Undoubtedly, humiliations and contempt are painful. They belittle us. Nevertheless, when we accept them with love and faith, they become God's *gift* of love and the *best way* to imitate the humble Heart of Jesus. Our Lord Jesus Christ suffered humiliation and rejection even before He was born. When Mary was about to give birth, there was no place for them at the Inn [87]. When Jesus

---

[87] Luke 2:6-7

was just a little babe, His family had to flee into Egypt because Herod was searching for Him to kill Him [88]. During Our Lord's public life (after His convincing preaching), in a derogatory way, the scribes and pharisees were "astounded" at His wisdom[89]— as if Jesus had never done or said anything worthy or bright ... Were the teachers and doctors of the Law not astounded at His wisdom, when at 12 years old He was found in the temple by His parents? On several occasions Jesus was about to be stoned to death,[90] and His enemies were constantly seeking to get rid of Him ... until they culminated their infamous chase with the ignominy of the Cross. In that moment, when Our Lord was facing so many outrages, He compared Himself to a worm: "But I am a worm, and no man; scorned by men, and despised by the people. All who see me mock at me, they make mouths at me, they wag their heads."[91] But the Lord's words are preceded by a beautiful praise! While Jesus was expressing His deep sorrow, He was also *praising* His Father, "Yet, You are holy, enthroned on the praises of Israel. In You our fathers trusted; they trusted and You delivered them. To You they cried, and they were saved; in You they trusted, and were not disappointed." [92] And this Psalm used by the Lord, concludes with the following words, "You who fear the Lord, *praise* him! ... For he has not despised or abhorred the affliction of the afflicted; and he has not hidden his face from him, but has heard, when he cried

---

[88] Matthew 2:13-14

[89] Matthew 13:55-57

[90] John 10:31

[91] Psalm 22:6-7

[92] Psalm 22:3-5

to him." [93] Jesus crucified, at the summit of pain and surrender—denying and ignoring Himself—*fully trusted* that His pain and humiliation were a source of *salvation.* For each one of us also, humiliations are the sure and straight path to eternity because "just as patience leads us to peace, and study to science; *humiliations* are the path which lead to humility"[94].

e. *To serve God in others.* Only the humble soul knows how to serve. To serve is not always easy; it requires effort and sacrifice. It is convenient to constantly remind ourselves that "if we do not live to serve, we are not worth living".

On March 18th, 2001, His Holiness, St. John Paul II, placing Saint Joseph as a beautiful example of humility and loving service, taught us that "St Joseph lived at the *service* of his Wife and Divine Son; for believers, he thus became an eloquent example of how 'to reign' is 'to serve'." *To reign is to serve!* Such a different lifestyle and way of thinking! We have constructed a *self-centered, selfish* society. We like to be served, to be catered, but God teaches us that we must serve as Jesus—and His earthly father Saint Joseph—did, with a humble and generous heart. We must serve God, especially in those who are nearest to us (our family members, our friends, and our neighbors), and we must also serve God in anyone who—though we do not know them personally—are in need. We must serve God in our brethren, independently of our Christian vocation and our busy schedule (in every state of life, profession, place, or time).

---

93 Psalm 22:23-24

94 Saint Bernard of Claraval. French Cistercian monk and Doctor of the Church.

How to achieve humility in our life? It is difficult to know, and even more difficult to *practice!* If it were easy, the world would be so different! But Jesus came to lead us to the Father. Let us contemplate Him and try to follow in His steps—though we know that those steps are painful and lead us to the cross. On the other hand, we also have the saints' example: common people who conquered themselves and their vices, until they reflected a certain aspect of the Lord's life and personality in their own lives.

If we consider *all* the saints, the *greatest* and *best* model to follow is the Blessed Virgin Mary. Amidst every single woman, of all ages, cultures, and social backgrounds—from the foundation to the end of the world—She was chosen to be the Mother of Almighty and Eternal God; and yet, She *always* remained the humble "handmaid of the Lord." [95] Let us pray to Mary every day, asking Her to obtain for us—from God—the grace of Her heart's humility. As Saint Augustine says, "It was pride that changed the angels into demons; it is humility which transforms men into angels." Let us also ask Our Blessed Mother to obtain for us all the other virtues which embellish Her soul, so that we may be able to please the Lord and fulfill the mission that He has entrusted to us.

Humility is one of the most powerful "keys" there could ever be. It opens the Heart of *God* and of *all* men. "God opposes the proud, but gives grace to the humble," [96] because the humble recognizes and takes responsibility for his own mistakes and does not blame them on anything or anyone else; and because He sees the Hand of God in every success and blessing he receives.

---

95 Luke 1:38

96 1 Peter 5:5.

Since we *cannot* achieve humility by ourselves, let us confidently allow the Lord to take our life in His hands—like the clay in the potter's hand[97]—so that He may shape us and help us to obtain this beautiful virtue. "Jesus, meek and humble of Heart, make our hearts like unto Thine," so that "dressed in brown," we may obtain from the Father the necessary graces to live in peace. Help us, Lord, to cooperate with these graces, so that one day we may get to Heaven—after having fulfilled the special mission and the dreams that you hold dearly in Your Heart for each one of us. "Jesus, meek and humble of Heart," grant us that being docile to Your Will, to Your commandments, and to Your lead—sometimes easy, but many other times mysterious and painful—we may come to the eternal embrace of Your glory. Amen.

---

[97] Jeremiah 18:4.

CHAPTER VI: The Ark

Noah's story is very well known: In order to save him from the universal flood, God sent this faithful man to build an *Ark*. Through this Ark, the Lord preserved Noah, his children, and pairs of animals of all the species that had existed from the beginning of Creation. When the Lord entrusted His good and obedient servant with this task. He gave him *precise* instructions on how to construct the saving vessel: the height, width, and length. The Almighty also specified every other measurement and material that *He* had chosen for the Ark [98]. Regardless of the difficulties and vicissitudes of this work, "Noah carried out all the commands that God gave him" [99].

After the flood Noah, his family, and the animals remained safe. The Lord, in His infinite Mercy, allowed them to come out of the Ark before they ran out of food. Indeed, the Lord saved them, but to do so, God desired to count on Noah's help: apart from the hard work involved in building the Ark—prior to the flood—God asked Noah to fill it up with provisions. Noah did his part by *always faithfully fulfilling* God's commands and indications. The result of his obedience is evident: he and his family received the Lord's abundant Blessings, and God began a "new creation" with them.

There is another Ark: *The Ark of the Covenant.* In Exodus, chapter 25, we can read how—due to its great importance—Moses received from God *precise* instructions on the details of its construction and assembly.[100] The Ark symbolized the love

[98] Genesis 6:14-16

[99] Genesis 6:22

[100] Exodus 25:10-21

and union between God and His chosen people. It was God's sanctuary and the means through which He instructed them, led them, and preserved them from danger and from the enemies that constantly assailed them. The Ark's transportation and care were reserved solely to the priestly tribe of the Levites. The sacred vessel protected them in battle and was an efficacious means to keep them away from idolatry since possessing it with them meant having God at their side. Thus, the Ark would always lead and precede the people: *God first!* For all the above, we can understand how, this second Ark, was also *extremely* important for the People of Israel!

There is yet a third Ark: according to the Fathers of the Church, the Blessed Virgin Mary symbolizes, in a mystical way, the *Ark of the New Covenant.* Jesus Christ, the Son of God, consubstantial with the Father, lived within Her for nine months. Since Our Lady is the perfect Ark, we will dedicate another chapter exclusively to Her.

For the moment I would like to speak about another "*Ark of the New Covenant*"*:* The institution of the *Holy Catholic Church.* This Ark is mainly (but not exclusively) *spiritual.* More than 2000 years ago, during His public life and after His Glorious Resurrection from the dead, Jesus carefully instructed His Apostles on how to build *HIS Church.*[101] As with the construction of the other Arks, the Lord gave His Apostles *precise* instructions on how to build it. Because the Catholic Church is the *Ark of the New Covenant*, the *REAL* presence of God in this Ark will remain with us "to the close of the age"[102].

---

[101] Matthew 16:18-19; Matthew 28:20

[102] Matthew 28:20

The wonder of *creation* was enclosed in *NOAH'S* Ark; it especially represented an unparalleled treasure: *human life,* made in the "image and likeness" of God.[103] The Ark *OF THE COVENANT* contained the two tablets of the Law, Aaron's rod, and a pot of manna [104], all of them symbols of the presence of God among them. In the Ark *OF THE NEW COVENANT* (the Holy Catholic Church), we find enclosed precious treasures, which help those who enter it, *to reach eternal salvation and to live intimately united with God.* These precious treasures are: The *real presence* of God in the Eucharist and His *sanctifying grace* in the other Sacraments, the maternal protection of the Blessed Virgin Mary, the guide of the Vicar of Christ, the Communion of Saints, and so much more!

It is important to remember that, to enter this sacred "Ark," we must receive the first of the Sacraments: Baptism. This sacrament is of vital importance. If we do not receive baptism, our soul *remains a total and open prey to the malignant,* and we are neither allowed into Heaven nor into the "Ark of the New Covenant"—the Ark of Salvation. But, once we are baptized, *we are placed in the loving arms of the Father,* we *obtain the outpouring of the Holy Spirit*, and we receive an *indelible mark* in our soul (which is called "*character*"). This character identifies us as children of God. It is the sign by which God recognizes us and by which He can "claim" us as *His* possession. It is essential to accept this free gift, the grace of this Sacrament ... and to accept the gift as soon as possible! Why leave our children as a prey to the

---

103 Genesis 1:26

104 Numbers 17:10

malignant, when they can enjoy such vital and marvelous favors just by being baptized? Let us never exchange what is essential for what is not important (for example, a big party to celebrate our little one's baptism).

We will dedicate the following lines to two other Sacraments: the Eucharist and the Sacrament of Penance (also known as Confession or Reconciliation). Receiving them with *faith and frequency* can greatly help us to obtain the *true happiness*. Through the *Eucharist*, which is the Body, Blood, Soul, and Divinity of Jesus Christ—*TRULY PRESENT AND ALIVE*—God remains *with* us and *within* us.

> *I will make a covenant of peace with them; it shall be an everlasting covenant ... and I will set my sanctuary in the midst of them for evermore. My dwelling place shall be with them; and I will be their God, and they shall be my people.* [105]

It is true that, when it comes to finding Jesus (really present and hidden in the Eucharist), our senses can deceive us. But even if our senses deceive us, the greatest and most marvelous *reality* is that— *despite* our limitations, which impede us to recognize Him—*Jesus is truly present and alive* in that little Consecrated Host. He awaits us in the Eucharist, ready to pour out all His love and grace over those who come to Him with a pure and humble heart. Let us pay close attention to what Saint Thomas Aquinas says in his Hymn, "Adoro te devote":

---

[105] Ezekiel 37:26-27

O Godhead hid, devoutly I adore Thee,
Who truly art within the forms before me;
To Thee my heart subjects and bows totally,
As it dissolves in contemplating Thee.

Sight, touch, and taste in Thee are each deceived;
The ear alone most safely is believed:
I believe all the Son of God has spoken,
That truth's own word there is no truer token;

God only on the cross lay hid from view;
But here lies hid at once the manhood too;
And I, in both professing my belief,
Make the same prayer as the repentant thief.

Thy wounds, as Thomas saw, I do not see;
Yet Thee confess my Lord and God to be;
Make me believe Thee ever more and more;
In Thee my hope, in Thee my love to store.

O Thou memorial of our Lord's own dying!
O living bread, to mortals' life supplying!
Make Thou my soul henceforth on Thee to live,
Ever a taste of heavenly sweetness give.

O loving Pelican! O Jesus Lord!
Unclean I am, but cleanse me in Thy Blood!
Of which a single drop, for sinners split,
Can purge the entire world from all its guilt.

Jesus, whom, for the present, veiled I see,
What I so thirst for, o! vouchsafe to me;
That I may see Thy countenance unfolding,
And may be blest Thy glory in beholding. Amen.

On a certain occasion I heard someone commenting that a Jewish gentleman said, "I do not understand how, if Catholics really believe that God is truly present in that piece of bread, the lines to receive Him aren't streaming out of their churches." This person was absolutely right! Sadly, faith in the *real presence* of Jesus in the Eucharist has been *lost!* Maybe this is the *worst* tragedy that has afflicted our world! How is it possible that Catholics waste the opportunity to receive God in our hearts as frequently as we can?! Can there be any other gift—in the entire universe—as marvelous and sublime as this one? *None* can compare to the mystery of God's presence within our soul!

If sometimes it seems difficult to participate and to focus during Mass, I would like to offer a few considerations. First, we can ask our Guardian Angel to come with us and to teach us to adore God like he adores Him. Then, it might be helpful to remember that freedom to come to Mass is a gift, and sadly, not every country offers this same liberty to their citizens! Another point to be considered is taking sufficient time to arrive in Church before Mass begins and not coming in a rush. If we arrive early, we will have enough time to prepare and to speak with the Lord "heart to Heart" before the Holy Sacrifice begins. On the contrary, if we arrive hastily, when the priest is already entering the Church in procession—and even worse—when Mass has already started, it will be very difficult for us to pay attention and to focus in the sacred mysteries (the preaching, death, and resurrection of the Lord—for love of each one of us).

It may happen that—even if we have arrived with plenty of time in advance and have sincerely tried to prepare for prayer—

we still get distracted at Mass, during prayer, or at adoration. We need to remember Saint Teresa of Avila, who used to call our imagination "the crazy lady of the house." Let us try to "come back" to the Lord as soon as we realize that we are distracted. Let us ask for forgiveness and for His grace so that we may be able to remain in His company. Let us continue "the battle" to be faithful, offering up the frustrations of this combat. Even when this struggle occupies all of our prayer time, this prayer is *also pleasing* to the Lord. He knows the depth of our soul and our many limitations. God does not ask for a *perfect* prayer but for a prayer full of *love.* Finally, we must never forget that we have the sweetest intercessor: Our Blessed Mother. Because we do not know how to pray, we can place our intentions in Her Immaculate Heart, and ask Her to present them before the Most Blessed Trinity.

The third commandment tells us, "You shall keep the Lord's Day holy." God has given us this commandment because He knows us and understands how much we are in need to be in communion (common-union) with Him. If there weren't one day during the week, in which we must stop and approach His altar, maybemanydays—orevenmonths…oryears—wouldpassbeforewe remembered our duty to adore Him. Yes, our Sunday obligation is a covenant. In this covenant we adore and thank the Lord. He, in turn, fills us with the graces and blessings we need to live a *God-filled* week. Sunday is "the Day of the Lord" and we must not forget it! During Mass, the same Mystery is celebrated for every *one of us*. Nevertheless, a Mass *well* lived centers us and brings us closer to the Lord. It fills us with blessings, strength, and peace. Conversely, a Mass poorly lived—unfortunately—does *not* have the same effect in our soul. What are some of the impediments to participating worthily at Mass? They include distractions of all types and to be anxiously waiting for Mass to be done—so that we can leave and do other activities—which will, most likely, make us forget about God (on His Day and throughout the week)!

Let us remember the example of the woman, who had suffered from a hemorrhage for twelve years. No doctor had been able to heal her. She believed in Jesus and went to Him. Just by touching the tassel of the Lord's cloak, she was totally and instantly healed of her illness [106]. If that occurred just by touching His garment, imagine the marvels that Jesus will do when we allow Him to come into our soul! His only desire is to make us happy and to set His dwelling place in us—*forever!* "The blessed Eucharist contains the whole spiritual good of the Church, namely *Christ* Himself." [107] For this reason, we should receive Jesus in Holy Communion with utmost love, reverence, devotion, humility, and gratitude. It is *God* Himself who comes down! We must recognize our unworthiness and revere Him for His infinite Mercy and love. We must remain in awe as we consider how is it possible that God—in all His Majesty—stoops down so low, but with so much love, to us, unworthy creatures! Let us allow enough time to adore the Most Blessed Trinity, truly present in our soul after communion. Let us remember that God remains in us *substantially* (His Body, Blood, Soul, and Divinity)—and we in Him—for fifteen minutes! Also, let us make an effort to visit Him frequently in the Most Blessed Sacrament. How generous of the

---

[106] Matthew 9:20-22

[107] Catechism of the Catholic Church - No. 1324.

Lord to remain exposed in the monstrance, and by doing so, brings us a little piece of Heaven! How sad when He lovingly *awaits* us, and He *can't* find committed adorers to give Him *an hour* of their time!

The Lord is our joy, *the true happiness*. Let us run to His encounter as often as we can and not waste the opportunity to obtain *the true happiness* given to us by the *presence of God!* Let us not despise this great *gift* of approaching the Lord (with deep love, fervor, and respect) in each Holy Communion and in every hour of adoration. Let us *adore* Him in the Blessed Sacrament, whether in Holy Communion or solemnly exposed in a Monstrance. In the Eucharist, Jesus is *humbly* hidden, but with *great power*. He awaits us to be our Companion, Guide, and Consolation. When we encounter Jesus in the Holy Eucharist, Our Lord fills us with His peace and with His infinite love!

The other sacrament that we will briefly mention, is the sacrament of penance. In it we find the treasure of God's *forgiveness* with *CERTAINTY* that we are truly being forgiven by Him! [108] What a beautiful and priceless reality! "Sin is before all else an offense against God, a rupture of communion with Him. At the same time, it damages communion with the Church."[109] Indeed, when we sin, we *painfully* offend God! With our sins, we also offend our brethren (the ones we see—and whom we directly hurt—and those whom we do not see, but who—as part of the mystical body of Christ—also become direct recipients of the consequences of our bad thoughts, decisions, words, and actions). However, since

---

108 John 20:21-23

109 Catechism of the Catholic Church - No. 1440.

God is a deeply compassionate and merciful Father, in confession He offers us sanctifying grace. This grace helps us to be better—as long as our soul is well disposed (with a *sincere* effort to *stop sinning*; with the desire to *do good*, to *love God* above all things, and to *love our neighbor* as ourselves). This is what the Most Blessed Trinity asks us to do and what Jesus taught us with His example: *to love and to do good.*

How beautiful and powerful is the sacrament of Penance: a sincere and humble confession can be a *true* exorcism! How much peace and joy it pours into our souls! Thank you, Lord, for offering us this great treasure, *freely!* Through a *good* confession You fill us with the hope of knowing that we can start anew and become *new creatures* more similar to You—even if we have fallen—only for being a part of your "Ark"!

To conclude this chapter, I would like to bring to mind once again, the fact that God gave *precise* instructions to His Apostles (especially to Saint Peter and his successors[110]) as to how to build and guide the Church of the "*new and everlasting* Covenant." [111] We must pray tirelessly and with filial love for the person whom God *legitimately* chooses to be His Vicar: The Holy Father. According to Jesus' words: "Whoever listens to you listens to Me. Whoever rejects you rejects Me. And whoever rejects Me, rejects the one who sent Me". [112]

We live in "flood" times. The rain is increasing, but we are navigating in a *safe* "Ark." The Catholic Church keeps us safe.

---

110 Matthew 16:18; Mark 4:24

111 Luke 22:20

112 Luke 10:16

Jesus promised that *He* would be with us through the centuries (in His Church and in His Sacraments) and Jesus does *not* lie! With Him at our side we are well because at the proper time—like in the time of Noah and in the time of the Apostles—God will calm the tempests! “And a great storm of wind arose, and the waves beat into the boat, so that the boat was already filling … He awoke and rebuked the wind, and said to the sea, ‘Peace! Be still!’ And the wind ceased, and there was a great calm” [113].

> *The world goes on its laborious way, proud of its riches, of its power, of its arms, of its genius; the Church goes onward along the course of ages with an even step, trusting in God only, to Whom, day and night, she lifts her eyes and her suppliant hands.*[114]

Let us *not* leave God’s Ark—despite the tempests, the thunderstorms, and the hailstones that slash it all over; in spite of the “dizziness,” the nausea, and the annoyances. If we persevere faithfully, at the end we will emerge out of it, to encounter Our God and faithful Friend Face to face—He, who has kept us safe in the journey of life—and *that* encounter will be *our true happiness FOREVER!*

---

[113] Mark 4,37-39

[114] Pope Leo XIII. *Octobri Mense*. Encyclical on the Rosary. September 22nd, 1891. No. 3.

CHAPTER VII: Lord, Give Me Patience, but Do It Now!

We have just reflected on Noah's example and how his fidelity to God allowed him to be a part of the "new Creation." God wants us to be a part of it too. But in order to achieve this, it is necessary that we—like Noah, Moses, and every one of the saints—may always carry out *all* of the Lord's commands.[115] The Lord's dream is that we are docile and allow *Him* to model us as clay in the potter's hands [116]. If we permit God to work in us, this *new creation* will be much *greater* than the former one. The Divine "handy work" models us through His Spirit, and the Sanctifier frees us from every attachment to the sinful inclinations that erase Our Lord's image within us.

Let us revisit Noah's example as a person of great patience and prudence. After withstanding a tempest for forty days and forty nights while being enclosed in a boat (not only with his family, but with many noisy and "smelly" animals), once the vessel ran aground on the Ararat, he waited for several weeks before leaving the embarkment. Even after the dove came back with the olive branch in its beak, he continued waiting … and waiting … and waiting … until he had *full certitude* that coming down from the ark would be safe. Noah had to wait—with prudence and patience—until the waters dried out.

How difficult it is to wait, and how easy it is to get frustrated and to start complaining! There are times in which our

---

115 Genesis 6:22

116 Jeremiah 18:1-10

prayer becomes like the petition of the person who told God: "Please, give me patience. But do it now!" Yet, we *must not* be like this with the Lord. God is God, and we are mere *creatures*. As we know, God always responds to our petitions: sometimes His answer is "yes," sometimes it is "no," sometimes it is "wait" ... and this waiting can last for years—literally speaking! Saint Monica prayed day and night for her son's conversion, and she didn't see the fruit of her prayers until a few months before her death. Most definitely, we must learn to wait, because ultimately, the end of the road becomes the beginning: the beginning of a marvelous eternity! "You need endurance to do the will of God and receive what He has promised." [117] The promise of a life in eternal bliss *cannot* be achieved neither in one day, nor in one year!

> *If it seems as if God is delaying His response, it is because He is preparing a better gift. He will not deny it to us. God retains what we are not ready to receive. He wants us to have an ardent desire for His most sublime gifts. Which means that we must pray always, without dismaying.*[118]

Patience is one of the virtues of the saints, but also a virtue practiced by all those who achieve their goals in life. Benjamin Franklin spoke about patience saying: "With patience and tranquility you can obtain everything ... and more." Isaac Newton, the great mathematician, physicist, and scientist, said: "If I have

---

[117] Hebrews 10:36

[118] Saint Thérèse of Lisieux. Doctor of the Church.

done invaluable discoveries, it has been more due to patience, than to any other talent." Amado Nervo, the Mexican poet, expressed with wisdom the hidden reality of our waiting: "Why do you wait impatiently for things to happen? If they are useless for your life, it is also *useless* to wait for them. If they are *necessary*, they will come, and will come at the proper time." Saint Pio of Pietrelcina said: "Patience is more perfect in the measure that it is *not* mixed with any anxieties and uneasiness".

To save us, God needs us to persevere in our efforts to be faithful *until the end*, because as Jesus told Peter, "The spirit indeed is willing, but the flesh is weak." [119] We might have the best intentions, but when things get tough, it is easy to "throw the towel" and say "That's enough! No more!" The Lord can *only* bless those who keep a sincere and constant battle for righteousness, because as Saint Augustine assured, "God, who created you without you, will not save you without you." [120] Jesus already gave *everything* (to the last drop of His Most Precious Blood) for our salvation; now it is our turn to live a life deserving of His sacrifice—if this is even possible! We must cooperate with divine *grace* and form our *will power, denying* ourselves *every* day.[121] We need to *patiently* await God's own time to reveal His plan of salvation for our life. Let us not desire to know what the future holds for us, "for tomorrow will be anxious for itself." [122]

There are people for whom—because of their quiet, peaceful, tranquil nature—it is easier to be patient. There are

---

[119] Matthew 26:41

[120] Saint Augustine, Bishop of Hippo, Sermon 169.

[121] Matthew 16:24

[122] Matthew 6:34

others, like the Apostles John and James, who because of their temper, were called "The Sons of thunder" by Our Lord [123]. Obviously, the latter must work "overtime" to achieve patience... But the good news is that to a higher degree of *difficulty* corresponds a higher degree of *merit!* And the best news of all is that we are *not alone* in this task! During one of his Wednesday General Audiences, Pope Saint John Paul II told us that, "The Spirit intervenes with a deep, continued action at every moment and in every aspect of the Christian life, in order to guide human desires in the *right* direction, which is the direction of *generous* love of God and neighbor..." [124] and he continued his teaching reminding us that, "… the Holy Spirit *strengthens the will*, making it possible for men to resist temptations and to conquer in the internal and external struggles, to defeat the power of evil and especially of satan …." [125] The Holy Father finished this reflection by stressing that "The Holy Spirit gives the Christian the strength of fidelity, *patience*, and perseverance on the path of goodness and in the struggle against evil" [126].

We may live through very difficult, uncertain, really "stormy" times. Even though Our Lord seems to be "asleep," we have the *certainty* that He is not. He will rise to calm down the winds and to bring about peace [127] through the inner strength given to us by the Holy Ghost. He only asks us to have faith, patience, and trust. When faced with difficulty, let us repeat frequently:

---

[123] Mark 3:17

[124] His Holiness Saint John Paul II- General Audience, Wednesday, June 26, 1991.

[125] Ibid.

[126] Ibid.

[127] Mark 4:35-41

"Jesus, I trust in You"[128] and "Come, Holy Ghost," and as St. Padre Pio taught us, let us "Pray, hope, and *don't worry*". The Lord's Divine Providence *never fails*.[129] Let us be patient and trust in Him! Pope John Paul I, in his short pontificate said:

> *...We will only be free to obtain our true greatness in the measure that we are capable of surrendering to the truth and to the redemptive love of God, judging everything only according to Him ... 'We rejoice in our sufferings, knowing that suffering produces endurance, and endurance produces proven character, and proven character, hope. Our Christian hope is rooted there; and in virtue of this certainty of a convinced faith, we have the right to act with peaceful confidence in every situation of our lives, in the controversy of opinions, and even in our personal sorrowful ordeals.* [130]

In the great trials and tribulations of our life, we need patience. For most people, these *great* occasions and ordeals will not be frequent—Thanks be to God! For this reason, it is highly important to cultivate the virtue of patience on a *day-to-day* basis. Our character and soul are formed and forged in our *daily life*. We need and must exercise virtue in the *small* things, if we wish to be virtuous when the great trials come... if they ever do! If we want to

---

[128] Saint Faustina Kowalska–Devotion to the Divine Mercy.

[129] Matthew 6:25-34

[130] Letter on the occasion of the 85 Catholic journeys in Germany, Katholikentag (September 13-17, 1978).

live in peace and make others happy, and if we want to achieve *the true happiness*, we need to practice virtue in our daily encounter with family, friends, and in the workplace.

Saint Francis de Sales offers us another good way to practice patience: "The best remedy I know against the sudden impulses of impatience is a *sweet and affable silence*." Silence when we feel insulted by others; but also, silencing our mind when it is anxiously seeking answers or action, and expecting things to be done or solved "yesterday" (in our life or in the lives of those around us).

The best model of patience: Jesus Himself, who being God, waited in a "hidden" life. First, in His Mother's womb for nine months. Once He was born, He had to "increase in wisdom and in stature, and in favor with God and man" [131] as any other boy. Our Lord did not wait for one week or a month, not even for five years, to begin His public life and His preaching of the Kingdom ... In the *silence* of a poor and common life, He waited for *thirty* years, until his "Hour" came [132]—the Hour marked by the Father, to bring to completion the salvation of the world. And what an Hour that was: betrayal, revilement, abandonment, flogging, spitting, thorns, nails, solitude, silence, the lance! ... In spite of all of these, Jesus was the *supreme*, the *most dignified* example of patience: "like a lamb led to the slaughter," He was silent and "opened not his mouth" [133].

The Blessed Virgin Mary is also worthy of mention in this chapter. Among many other events that prove Her patience, let us

---

131 Luke 2:52

132 John 2:4

133 Isaiah 53:7

recall the Presentation in the Temple. When Jesus was just 8 days old, Mary heard from Simeon the prophecy that a sword would pierce Her heart.[134] Before this prophecy was fulfilled, She had to wait and suffer much (to be exact, for *thirty-three* years), but She remained always faithful, *without* questioning any of the events—and also the *uneventfulness*—of those many years. She always lived as "the handmaid of the Lord," [135] even at the foot of the Cross. There, in the moment when the prophecy was being fulfilled and a sword pierced Jesus' heart, it pierced Hers too, to the *deepest* fiber of Her being.[136] In that moment, Mary—spiritually—was *dying* alongside Her Beloved Son!

I would like to close this chapter with Saint Teresa of Avila's words: "Let nothing disturb you, let nothing frighten you, God never changes, *PATIENCE* ACHIEVES ALL THINGS..." Only the person who knows how to wait and endure achieves great things, but the *greatest* one of all: *eternal life*, *the true happiness*!

---

[134] Luke 2:35

[135] Luke 1:38

[136] John 19:31-34

CHAPTER VIII: Liberally

If you have climbed a mountain, and as you made it to the summit you have been able to contemplate the majesty that can only be experienced from the top; if you have walked in a forest, and listened to the murmur of a stream or the singing of the birds; if you have experienced a cool breeze in a hot day, and the crisp morning air; if you have sown a tiny seed and have seen ravishing flowers or fruits grow; if you have departed on an airplane and "landed" on the Hudson River and saw every crew member and all the passengers of your flight walk out alive [137]; if you have traveled uncountable times and have always left and come back home without any casualties ... You have already experienced God's generosity. But if you are a father or a mother, you are better able to understand the Lord's liberality: God—being the *Best Father*—offered His *Only* Son, His *Beloved* Son, to *die* for our salvation. What an unfathomable mystery!

Jesus walked, preached, and performed miracles. He finished His journey on Earth by giving His life on the Cross out of love. He, who is so infinitely generous, tells us, "Be perfect as your Heavenly Father is perfect." [138] Are we fulfilling His desires? Do we strive to live Christian perfection, as a sign of our love and obedience to God? Do we respond to His magnanimity, by being magnanimous towards others? ... What is Christian perfection? How can we live it?

---

137 "Miracle on the Hudson". US Airways flight 1549.

138 Matthew 5:48

We just heard the answer: "Be perfect as your Heavenly Father is perfect." If you are thinking "I cannot be like God," I congratulate you! Saint Michael, the Archangel, already cried out, "Who is like unto God, No one is like unto God!" Indeed, *NO ONE WILL EVER BE LIKE GOD!* Nevertheless, my dear friend, this invitation to be perfect—like our Heavenly Father is perfect—came from Jesus Christ (God, the Son of God). If He is placing the rod so high, it is because *He wants us to aim high!* The Lord knows us, and He understands that is necessary for us to have noble goals. We *cannot* be satisfied only with the things that we can do, because—aided by His grace—we will always be able to do more! Saint Paul said: "I am what I am by the grace of God" [139]. Through God's grace, one of the ways in which we can try to "be perfect" is by imitating the Lord in the virtue of *generosity*. Trying to be generous is a way in which we can acknowledge—and become a reflection (though pale)—of the Lord's bounty:

A) Generosity in giving. Saint Jose Maria Escriva taught us,

> *My children, wherever you find your brethren; anywhere you find your aspirations, your work, your loved ones, that is the place of your daily encounter with Christ. It is in the midst of the worldliest things that we must be sanctified by serving God and all men.*[140]

---

[139] 1 Corinthians 15:10

[140] Saint Jose Maria Escriva. Homily pronounced at the University of Navarra, October 8, 1967.

There are many ways in which we can practice generosity in giving during our "daily encounter with Christ":

a. *Generosity in giving material goods.* "Blessed are the poor in spirit, for theirs is the Kingdom of Heaven." [141] True poverty does not consist in the amount or lack of *possessions*, but in the heart's disposition to *share* them. "The person whose heart is full of love, will *always* have something to give" [142].

How beautiful it is to find in our lives people who give liberally! They become true instruments of Divine Mercy to us. They fill us with consolation and offer us their unconditional aid in the moments in which we most need them. How sad it is—on the contrary—to find people who are absorbed in themselves and obsessed with their own plans and businesses. They are so engrossed in earning that they take advantage of everything and everyone—even in the smallest opportunities. These people are so worried about increasing their profits, making great enterprises, and "filling their pockets," that they become blind to the needs of others. If they ever cooperate in a good cause, they either "sound the trumpet before them"[143] or are eternally embittered for what they have given ... Can we really blame them? We have *free will* and are *totally* responsible for our choices and conduct. Nevertheless, this attitude of avarice may be the fruit of the egotistic society in which we live. We are taught to place ourselves "at the top" and "at the center of the universe." We end up believing

---

141 Matthew 5:3

142 Saint Augustine. Bishop of Hippo. *Commentaries on the Psalms* (2nd. commentary on psalm 36, No.13).

143 Matthew 6:2

that *everything* is about *ourselves*, *our* plans, and *our* choices. But we must strive to live according to the *truth*: "the richest person is not the one who has the most, but the one who *least* desires." Society and the mass media "bombard" us with ideas related to how good it is to have and to have even more. We cannot allow ourselves to be *fooled* by the desire of possessing, believing that if we have more, we will be happier or more important before others. This is a lie! The pleasure of possessing lasts for an *instant;* giving lavishly produces *lasting happiness,* because to the one who "seeks *first* the Kingdom of God and His righteousness, *all* things will be added" [144].

Has it ever happened to you that after a few days or months of having bought a new car you find a scratch on it, the engine fails, or someone crashes into your vehicle? Or maybe you purchased a piece of clothing which you liked a lot, you washed it, and it shrank, or it came out of the washer or dryer with a spot or a tear? These are just simple examples that help us remember that the things of this world last for only a *brief* moment. The happiness they provide is just *ephemeral;* it vanishes with just a blow, in the twinkling of an eye.

The Roman poet Juvenal said: "Living poorly to die rich, is great madness." We must remember that we neither have the future nor life assured, and that *no one* will bring his riches to the tomb. We must keep in mind that the only thing that belongs to us is *today,* the *now;* that is why it is called "the present." God offers it to us, so that anything we do for the least of our brethren, we

---

[144] Matthew 6:33

do it for *Jesus* Himself.[145] *TODAY* is the time God is giving us to do *good,* to *be* good. Hopefully, it won't happen to us like in the Gospel story (found in Luke 12:15-21): A man accumulated riches, keeping them in his barns. The night when he thought he was ready to enjoy life "as much as he wanted," he was called by the Lord.[146] Where did all his reaches end? We don't know! Saint Paul, in his first letter to Timothy, warns us against avarice: "Those who desire to be rich fall into temptation, into a snare, into many senseless and hurtful desires, that plunge men into ruin and destruction. For the love of money is the root of all evils…" [147]

Generosity exalts us, makes us happy, and liberates us. Avarice destroys us: It does not allow us to enjoy even the things we already possess! "The poor man is lacking many things; the avaricious, *all.*" [148] As Saint Bernard explains it, "avarice is living in poverty, for fear of poverty." And according to Bion of Smyrna, "The avaricious man does not possess his richness, but these possess him" [149] and do not allow him to *share* with others.

Finally, I quote Saint Augustine's invitation: "Give what you have, so that you may deserve to receive what you are still lacking." We are all lacking, and we are lacking *a lot!* Let us become "experts" in detachment and in generosity for love of God, so that we may be ready to receive *all* the beautiful gifts that God has prepared for us.

---

145 Matthew 25:31-46

146 Luke 12:13-21

147 1 Timothy 6:9

148 Publio Siro (Latin writer of the Ancient Rome).

149 Bion of Smyrna (the last Greek bucolic poet).

b. *Generosity in giving love and understanding.* Loving—as a reflection of God's love for each one of us means: a sacrificial, total, absolute, an unbounded love. Saint Vincent de Paul willed to be a testimony of this love and to be present among his brethren by sharing God's tenderness. Saint Francis de Sales, his good friend, is also renowned for the immense sweetness with which he addressed others—even those who opposed him, his faith, and his points of view—and by his kindness towards the poor and the sick. Mother Teresa of Calcutta said that the United States of America is one of the poorest countries she ever visited because in this country she had found uncountable souls who were living in solitude and abandonment. Pope Saint John Paul II taught us, "[He] … is generous because He loves, and loving means being *lavish*, it means giving. It means being a gift, *being for others*, being for *all*, being for each and every one." [150] We must be generous in our love—for the poor, for the rich, for the young, for the elderly, etc.—because the *greatest* poverty is the *absence of love*, the *deficiency of affection.*

B) *Generosity in our words*. It is really easy to "make firewood of the fallen tree," to mercilessly "tear to pieces" a person who has made a mistake, who has a weakness or a defect. On the other hand, it is far more *beautiful* to "raise" the "fallen" (cheering him up, supporting him, defending him, speaking well of him, trusting him). Generosity in our words implies praising the qualities and virtues of others, avoiding anything that could damage their image or their reputation, and preventing any type of humiliation ... And

---

[150] Angelus –August 3, 1986.

if we believe that we have "nothing positive" to say, we can offer our generosity by keeping silent. Let us remember the example of the "plucked-feathered chicken" given to us by St. Philip Neri: if we collect the feathers and throw them from the top of a mountain on a windy day, it is impossible to pick all of them up afterwards! The same thing happens with our words: once they are out of our mouth, they do not come back to us without having been scattered all over the place. With words, the mass media manipulates and controls the public opinion, and it is enough for us to say something "small" to become "mass media" (manipulating and controlling information that does not belong to us). Saint James the Apostle says,

> *So the tongue is a little member and boasts of great things. How great a forest is set ablaze by a small fire! And the tongue is a fire. The tongue is an unrighteous world among our members, staining the whole body ... a restless evil, full of deadly poison. With it we bless the Lord and Father, and with it we curse men, who are made in the likeness of God.*[151]

If we want to find the *true happiness*, we must try to *always speak kindly* of others. Jesus taught us to speak always well of those who love us, but also of those who harm us: "... bless those who curse you." [152] "Speaking well is greatly favorable to our

---

[151] James 3:5-9

[152] Luke 6:28

society: it helps its edification, it lifts on high the person's dignity, and fills it with positive aspects." [153] Let us edify and build a *positive* society word by word, person by person!

Briefly, but not least importantly, another aspect of the generosity in our words is *sincerity.* Jesus said, "For this I was born, and for this I have come into the world, to bear witness to the truth." [154] Every time we lie—in a way—we disdain the mystery of the Incarnation (the loving sacrifice of God made flesh to save us, and to show us the way to the Father)! We should *never* lie! Lying is a grave sin—even when nowadays it is not given the importance it really deserves! "To assent to obvious lies is in some small way to become evil oneself." [155] We should never deceive others with our words, actions, or appearances—especially if we are insincere, *just* to obtain what we desire. Let us admit it: pretending to be rich, intelligent, or simulating a sex discordant to that given to us by God, will never make us happy! Full joy comes into our lives *only* when we accept with gratitude, humility, and joy the person we are and the things we can have. Let us live happily and gratefully for the gift of our creation and for the things we can obtain as the fruit of our honest labor and effort. "Transparency" in our life (lived in full submission to God's most Holy Will) will greatly benefit those that we encounter in our daily life, but also the whole society. It will make us deeply happy—because as it is prayed at the beginning of Mass in the Traditional rite—light and truth guide

---

[153] Christian Fabrizio Andrade-Virtues and values.

[154] John 18:37

[155] Theodore Dalrymple. English critic and psychiatrist, born in 1949. Many of his works are based on his work with criminals and mentally ill people.

us to God's dwelling places,[156] and *the true happiness* is only found in *Heaven*, which is God's dwelling place, where we will see *Him* face to face.

C) *Generosity in service*. There are some people who, taught by a good mother, have learned to serve when they were very little; in them, "lending a hand" springs naturally. This is beautiful and laudable. It is of vital importance that in them—and in us—this service may spring not as a habit, but as the consequence of a deep connection of our heart with God's Heart. The Lord invites us to *do good* with firm confidence, because when we aid someone, it is *God* whom we serve. [157]

To achieve this union with the Lord—which brings us to a sincere and selfless service—it is necessary to appreciate *silence* and *prayer*. When the soul lives in deep union with God, generous service springs up naturally. We can see this clearly reflected in the example of the Blessed Mother. There is very little written about Her in the Gospels, yet, most of the times when Mary is mentioned, we find Her serving. After receiving the message of the Archangel Gabriel at the Annunciation, Our Lady—knowing that She was going to be the Mother of God, and in spite of the inconveniencies caused by the first trimester of pregnancy (nausea, dizziness, etc.....)— "...went *in haste* to the hill country" [158] to *help* and *serve* Her cousin Elizabeth—who in her old age—was also expecting a baby. At the wedding feast of Cana, the Blessed Virgin

156 "Emitte lucem tuam et veritatem tuam: ipsa me deduxerunt, et adduxerunt in montem sanctum tuum, et in tabernacula tua".

157 Matthew 25:40

158 Luke 1:39

Mary was the *first* one to notice the bridal couple's need. Our Lady tried to solve their problem and to be of *service* by *interceding* for them before Jesus. Mary had *full certitude* that Her Son would be able to help them! Finally, Mary, as the best follower of Jesus, truly lived the Gospel "… Should anyone press you into service for one mile, go with him for two miles." [159] The Blessed Virgin Mary is the best example of the type of generous service that Jesus asks from us. Our Lady shows us how to give more than what we "ought," to give far beyond that which is expected from us. Mary teaches us to serve *always* (in every moment and circumstance) and to do it with *joy* and *kindness.* She instructs us so that we may be attentive and understand the needs of others—even before we are asked for help.

Finally, let us remember that in order to serve, we must forget about ourselves. Part of this *self-denial* is to depart from criticism, which—as we have seen—is so destructive and harmful. Criticizing places a "barrier," which prevents us from having cordial and kind human relationships.

D) <u>*Generosity in forgiveness*</u>. In the second chapter of this book, we mentioned the importance of forgiveness as a facet of love. Now we will analyze other forms of generosity in forgiveness. First: forgiving *without* demanding anything in return. "Forgiveness in its highest and truest form, is an act of free love." [160] Forgiving with generosity implies forgiving with our heart, but also with our will, memory, and intelligence. Many times, "forgiving is not forgetting. Forgiving is the generous remission of a debt that may never be

[159] Matthew 5:41

[160] His Holiness John Paul II – Offers forgiveness, receives peace. XXX Day for World Peace, December 8, 1996, n 5.

paid off." [161] Mother Teresa of Calcutta wisely taught us that "to forgive we need *love*, and to forget we need *humility*".

While Jesus was hanging on the Cross, He said, "Father, forgive them, for they know not what they do." [162] A generous forgiveness, *justifies!* When we are "nailed" on our "cross," and it is hard to give a generous forgiveness, let us turn our eyes to Jesus Crucified and humbly ask Him: "Jesus, it is very difficult for me to forgive, but there is nothing impossible for You, please help me to forgive!" The Lord—who sees and knows all things, and who loves us profoundly—perfectly understands everything that we have experienced and our present circumstances. He, who is faithful, will generously help us with the *grace* of forgiveness if we ask Him with a *sincere* and *humble* heart.

Generosity in forgiveness will help us to "make a truce" with the person who has offended us. It will also give us great inner peace—a type of peace that the world cannot give because it can only come from God.[163] "The world *cannot* give Christ's peace." [164] And we cannot forget that "The measure you give, will be the measure you get back, and still more will be given to you." [165] We must forgive "abundantly", without "storing" anything (rancor, grudges, or ill-feelings), so that we may receive from the Lord His *generous* forgiveness. We need to keep always in mind that, as we mentioned before, forgiveness is the only grace that we receive as

---

[161] Truqui, Cesar. *Secretos para Perdonar de Corazón*, Editorial el Arca, S.A. de C.V., México, D.F., 2008

[162] Luke 23:34

[163] John 14:27

[164] His Holiness Benedict XVI-Mass on the Solemnity of Pentecost, May 11, 2008.

[165] Mark 4:24

an *exchange* for our actions. Jesus said: "If *you* forgive men their trespasses, your heavenly Father *also* will forgive you; but if you *do not* forgive men their trespasses, *neither* will your Father forgive your trespasses." [166] Let us reflect on the Lord's words, and ask Him for the grace of a *humble* heart that *always* forgives with generosity!

E) *Generosity in suffering*. We live in a "valley of tears." Everyone, in some way or another, experiences sorrow and suffering in this life. It is inevitable, and part of our fallen nature. However, "man in a special fashion becomes the way for the Church, when suffering enters his life" [167]. There are some chosen souls—who amid the greatest physical and/or spiritual sufferings—continue loving, praising, blessing, and glorifying God. Saint Andrew Apostle, after hanging on the cross of his martyrdom for two days, exclaimed before his death,

> *Lord, eternal King of glory, receive me hanging from the wood of this sweet cross. Thou who art my God, whom I have seen, do not permit them to loosen me from the cross. Do this for me, O Lord, for I know the virtue of Thy Holy Cross.*

Like Saint Andrew, there have been hundreds of souls—who are unknown to the world—but who have endured their pain and suffering with deep love, absolute surrender, and extreme

---

[166] Matthew 6:14

[167] His Holiness Saint John Paul II-Encyclical Letter Salvifici Doloris-No. 3.

generosity. This is the kind of generosity—humble, but heroic—which makes God's Heart "beat" and that touches the inner depths of His Being. Generosity in suffering keeps us *all* alive: the Lord has Mercy on the whole world out of love for *these suffering souls!* Those who are heroically generous in suffering earn merits of eternal salvation for an uncountable number of people who are greatly benefited by their love, surrender, and humble acceptance of God's Will. "Human suffering has reached its culmination in the Passion of Christ. And at the same time, it has entered into a completely new dimension and a new order: *it has been linked to love...*" [168] and thus, generosity in suffering becomes a way to the *true happiness*.

It is *very important* to respond to the suffering souls' generosity, with *our own* generosity: supporting them in any way we can (while they are still suffering among us) and praying for them after their death (even when we think that they are in Heaven). If these souls are already resting in the Lord, our prayers will go to someone else who needs them to obtain the total purification required to enter into the Lord's eternal rest.

F) Generosity in joy. A person who smiles puts a smile on the face of others. Even if we do not realize it, we are "mirrors" of the people and of the circumstances that surround us. As they say: "life is a boomerang." Whatever we throw into the air will come back at us! If we wish for people to be nice, let us be nice *first*.

---

[168] His Holiness Saint John Paul II-Encyclical Letter Salvifici Doloris- No. 18.

Let us be generous in joy by speaking positively, saying words that will uplift others and that will make them feel loved and important. Let us be generous in joy trying to foster always *friendly* and *positive* environments. Let us be the first to congratulate whoever has obtained a prize, an acknowledgment, a raise in salary, or a promotion at work. *Rejoicing* with the well-being of others is generosity in joy. The person who strives to be generous in joy ends up finding *the true happiness* because most of the people desire to share time and experiences with the person who is joyfully generous. Whoever brings joy to others *will not be lonely*!

As we walk through the path of life, Jesus invites us to take advantage of every opportunity to generously love and serve Him in the love and service of our brethren. He reminds us: "Give and it will be given to you; a good measure, pressed down, shaken together, running over, will be put into your lap." [169] The reward is marvelous and beyond all telling! The person who loves *generously* and who gives *unceasingly* will be awarded with holiness of life and friendship with God—on this Earth and after this life, in Heaven where he will contemplate the Lord Face to face, in all His Beauty and splendor, *forever*!

May the Most Blessed Trinity help us to give "liberally"—to those who are near and far, to those whom we know, and to those we don't—so that He, who is infinite Goodness and Generosity, may transform our life into a bright path that will lead many to the encounter with the Lord. May God's grace and love be always our strength and—through a mutual exchange of love—may Jesus make our light break forth like the dawn, heal our wounds, lead

---

[169] Luke 6:38

our way, and make us strong to do what is good and to be always pleasing in His eyes.[170] Amen.

170 Isaiah 58:6-14.

CHAPTER IX: God is Stronger!

On the 13th of October 1884, Pope Leo XIII had the following vision:

> *I saw devils and heard their gnashing, blasphemies, and mockery. I heard satan's horrifying voice defying God, saying that he could destroy the Church, and bring the whole humanity into hell, if he were given enough time and power. Satan asked God for permission to have 100 years, in which he could freely influence the world, as he had never done before.*

After this vision, the Pope could also see Saint Michael the Archangel appearing and casting satan and his legions back into the abyss of hell. This is how the prayer to Saint Michael was written, a prayer which Pope Leo XIII asked us to pray *every day* after the Holy Mass:

> *Saint Michael the Archangel, defend us in battle; be our defense against the wickedness and snares of the devil; may God rebuke him, we humbly pray, and do Thou, O Prince of the Heavenly Hosts, by the Divine power of God, cast into hell Satan and all the other evil spirits who prowl about the world seeking the ruin of souls. Amen.*

If we have lost this tradition, it might be a good moment to reinstate it: the devil "has come down … in great wrath, because he knows that his time is short." [171] The evil one is unleashed, and rabidly snatching away souls into hell—wishing to drag with his tail, as many as he possibly can. He does not "discriminate" by age, sex, or color. He wants us *all*, rotting in hell with him!

"Be sober and watchful. Your adversary the devil prowls around like a roaring lion, seeking someone to devour." [172] This fallen angel is merciless and wicked; he does not "touch his heart" because he does not have it. No, he does not have a heart, he does not have an inch of love within him. According to Saint Teresa of Avila, "if satan could love, he would stop being wicked." [173] This evil spirit *rejoices in our sorrow*. He lies—making us believe that he will grant goods—only to proceed to the "plucking out of the eyes" and to leave people in the *deepest depression* and *emptiness*. He comes to bring division, doubt, rancor, and confusion. Depriving us from peace is his favorite work! That is why we must "resist him, steadfast in faith" [174] and be *very* vigilant. We must be really watchful: *pray and make sacrifices,* because "there are some demons that can only be driven away by prayer and fasting." [175] We cannot get discouraged when faced with trials. We must keep going on—remaining faithful to God—because He has called us and predestined us to *eternal salvation*. "And after you have

171 Revelation 12:12

172 1 Peter 5:8

173 Saint Teresa de Ávila. Doctor of the Church.

174 1 Peter 5:9

175 Matthew 17:21

suffered a little while, The God of all grace, who has called you to his eternal glory in Christ, will himself restore, establish, and strengthen you." [176] We must *not* dismay if it seems that our efforts and prayers are in vain, because they *are not. I*f it were like that, Jesus would *not* have died on the Cross.

> *Sacrifice is the inseparable complement to prayer; and is all the more effective, if generous. The suffering ... of those united in a special manner on the way of the Cross with Jesus, Redeemer of every man and of the whole man, gains an immeasurable value.*[177]

For this reason, we must "put on the armor of God": obedience, truth, humility, justice, faith, the Word of God, and prayer. This armor will help us to courageously proclaim the Gospel of peace.[178] If God grants us the grace to help out in the salvation of at least one soul—from the claws of the enemy and from the terrors of hell—all our efforts and sacrifices will seem like nothing compared to the great joy of having been able to help the Lord to find His "lost sheep". "When you work for Christ and with Christ, you labor for justice, peace and a development that are not ideological but *real*, thus helping to build the civilization of love"[179] … and an *eternal* City.

---

[176] 1 Peter 5:10

[177] St. Pope John Paul II – Message for the World Day of Missions, 1994 – No. 4.

[178] Ephesians 6:13-18

[179] St. Pope John Paul II – Message for the World Day of Missions, 1994. No. 2.

In the passage of the paralytic's friends, we discover the type of love and faith which moves the person into action. In their desire to help the paralytic, his friends tried everything possible—even to the point of removing the roof of a house—to place their friend before Jesus, hoping that the Lord would heal him.[180] God has placed us on Earth to help and pray for others. Also, we are here to be aided by the intercession of our good friends: earthly and Heavenly friends. We are not alone in our battle against evil. We have people who pray for us, but above all, we count on the faithful help of the Lord. A very important means through which He gives us this help is the most powerful and sweet aid that we receive through the mediation of the Blessed Virgin Mary, Saint Joseph, all the Saints and Angels, and by *sanctifying* grace (received when we participate in the Sacraments of His Church and when—with God's help—we *actively* and *decisively* try to avoid and reject sin in our daily life).

Like the paralytic's friends, let us try to be good friends of Our God and of our brethren. If our love is truthful, we will toil *unceasingly*, seeking for the greatest number of souls to know and love the Lord; we will work restlessly, until the whole world may repeat with Saint Augustine:

> *Late have I loved You, O Beauty ever ancient, ever new, late have loved You! You were within me, but I was outside, and it was there that I searched for You. In my unloveliness, I plunged into the lovely things which You created. You were with me, but*

---

180 Mark2:3-4

> *I was not with You. Created things kept me from You; yet if they had not been in You, they would not have been at all. You called and cried out, and You broke through my deafness. You shone and were resplendent, and You dispelled my blindness. You exhaled your fragrance; I inhaled it, and now I sigh for You. I have tasted You, now I hunger and thirst for You. You touched me, and I was set ablaze in Your peace.*[181]

"A man who is *distant from God is also distant from himself*, alienated from himself, and *can only find himself by encountering God.*" [182] Thus, when a soul is intimately and deeply united to the Lord, all of his work —even the smallest and most " insignificant"—becomes a pleasing offering, like "incense" that raises up to Heaven and gives glory to God. If our heart is firmly adhered to God, we should not be afraid of our soul's enemy because *GOD IS, AND WILL EVER BE STRONGER!* God is God, and the devil is just a mere creature—who *must* obey the commands of the Creator and King of the Universe, of Almighty and eternal God—whether he likes it or not. If we are on God's side, we are assured victory because *God is stronger* and, in the end, HE WILL TRIUMPH!

---

[181] Confessions X, 27, 38.

[182] His Holiness Benedict XVI –General Audience – Wednesday, January 30, 2008.

CHAPTER X: United Forever!

We live in a society of waste, materialism, and utilitarianism: "If I like it and can use it, then, I want it; if I can't, I trash it." Has this attitude been also adopted when choosing a girlfriend? A wife? It causes affliction to understand that many young couples approach marriage without real preparation, without a thoughtful consideration about the depth and greatness of the nuptial union. They make *the most vital decision of their lives* thinking, "If it works, we continue; if it doesn't, we get divorced. No big deal!" Young people who act like this do not realize the grave mistake into which they are falling! A divorce shatters the couple, their children, and society itself. As the Holy Father, Saint John Paul II said, "The family is the base of society and the place where people learn for the first time the values which will guide them along their life." If the family is weak, the *whole society* is weak, since "it is in the home where a better world is built."[183]

If we dream of a better world, it is in our hands to achieve it! We have the possibility to start building it through trust in God and our daily decisions. Each *small* choice we make—even those which seem most insignificant—make us a better or a worse person. This is extremely serious! If we opt for sacrifice, love, surrender, service, faith, and unlimited obedience to God's Will (in each one of our decisions), we will be righteous and happy and our life will be meaningful because we will constantly make *others* happy. What a challenge! Living like this is not easy. This is why

[183] Homily of St. Pope John Paul II -"Estadio del Sentro Deportivo Korsou"- Willemstad (Sunday May 13th, 1990- No. 5).

we must beg God to give us His grace *every day*, remembering the words of the Lord to Saint Paul, "My grace is sufficient for you, for my power is made perfect in weakness." [184] It is true, we are weak and without God we can do *nothing*, but *everything* is possible with God! [185] On the contrary, if our decisions are always centered on *ourselves* (on what we want and what *we* like; on that which offers us *momentary* gratification), in the long run we will be *hopeless*. We will make the lives of others deeply *unhappy.* People who live for themselves are *never* satisfied; nothing seems to be good enough for them; nobody will ever make them happy! Everyone will try everything possible to help them, to bring joy and motivation to their life, but there is no medicine that can heal a person who lives enclosed in himself. Sadly, he will be eternally dissatisfied! If God gives us the grace to understand that we might be one of these people—for our own sake and for the benefit of those we love (and who love us)- we need to come out of our "shell"! *God is infinitely Good, life is good and beautiful,* and it has many *amazing* things in store for us … We just need to *open* our eyes and our heart to the *many blessings* that surround us! Let us *be happy*, my dear friend, it is in *our* hands and in *no one* else's! "Do not allow anything or anyone to snatch away from you your trust in Him and your enthusiasm to build a new world, in which *generosity* and *love* will reign."[186] So that together we may do whatever is in our hands to achieve our dreams of a better world, let us share some ideas with the single people, with married couples, and with families.

[184] 2 Corinthians 12:9

[185] Luke 1:37

[186] Address of St. Pope John Paul II to the Youth. Willemstad, May 13th, 1990 – No. 6.

A) *For single people*. We must consider living with *purity, humility, and charity.* These are *our* "keys" to open the gates of Heaven and of *every* human heart. These virtues offer us a special aid to live and act with moderation and grace, and to make prudent decisions. Let us ponder their benefits because whoever tries to live with purity, humility, charity, moderation, prudence, and in grace, seems to navigate through the waters of life with more *ease* and *peace*. People who practice these virtues learn to choose good over evil; they are able to distinguish—among many women—the best wife; most importantly they know how to select *day by day* the path that will bring them safely to the final goal (to our eternal destiny and Home, which is Heaven).

Another very important virtue to practice is modesty. "Either we must speak as we dress, or dress as we speak. Why do we profess one thing and display another? The tongue talks of chastity, but the whole body reveals impurity." [187] In our actions and whenever we choose our words and clothing, let us always opt for decency. A good man is *never* trying to show, see, or do more than what he is allowed to, according to his state in life; neither does he speak disagreeable words, which degrade him as a person and as a child of God. "Filthy talk makes us feel comfortable with filthy actions. But the one who knows how to *control the tongue* is prepared to resist the attacks of lust." [188] If we show respect for ourselves, others will respect us. We must consider how if a girl is accepted by a young man—even when she always acts and

---

[187] Saint Jerome (342 A.D-420 A.D). Doctor of the Church. Translator of the Bible into Latin.

[188] Saint Clement of Alexandria. (150 A.D-215 A.D) Father of the Church.

dresses *modestly*—it is very likely that this young man will always see and treat her with *respect and dignity* (and not as a mere object of pleasure). Saint Augustine gives us the most important key to choose a good spouse: "If you want to know a person, don't ask him what he thinks, but rather what he loves." The good person loves, respects, hopes, and puts *God* first, always, everywhere, and in every circumstance. After God, he will put you, your eternal salvation, your happiness, and your well-being. After God and you, the good person will put others (especially those who are in need) next—leaving himself, his preferences, and his desires at last.

If a man wishes to know if the woman he is dating is good, he must pay attention to the way in which she deals with others (children, youth, and elderly; rich and poor; people of different races; people who are advanced in holiness and those who are starting their way to Heaven; the good and bad; those who treat her well and those who offend her; those who agree with her opinions and those who differ; the good drivers and those who are not, etc.) "Neither hate men for their vices nor hate vices because of men … hate in them that, for which they are iniquitous, and love that for which they are men." [189] If the person this young man is dating respects *everyone*—and treats them with charity, dignity, and patience—this shows that she has a big, open, and humble heart (and it is very likely that this girl will be willing to deal with him in the same way). On the other hand: if she is aggressive, disrespectful, or simply indifferent towards other people, it is very likely that she will treat him in the same way.

Also, appearance, conversation, and external manners are

[189] Saint Augustine, Bishop of Hippo. *Commentaries on the Psalms*, No. 138,28.

good indicators of who and how is the person we are dating. What we see outside is a reflection of the content that lays inside. We need to remember that men must look and act like men, like Saint Joseph: always manly, clean, courageous, intelligent, hard-working, detached from himself, humble, prudent, simple, faithful, charitable, and loving. And a woman must look and act like a woman, following the example of the Blessed Virgin Mary: always feminine, clean, tender, sweet, humble, simple, charitable, prudent, dedicated, laborious, diligent, caring, loving, and faithful. Whoever tries to practice these virtues, according to their own—God-given—sex, gives glory to his Creator. With humility, we must always repeat: "Lord, *You* have created me and you have chosen everything in me! Let me be the person that *You* want me to be!"

By God's design,[190] a couple's love must be *pure* and *only* between a man and a woman. Conjugal love is *sacred* and only beautiful when it is lived within marriage. "Free" love does not bring unity, but brokenness. It neither leads to salvation, nor to the *true happiness*. It only gives an instant of pleasure and many sorrowful consequences—like the loss of dignity, integrity, and self-esteem. It can also lead to depression and to "chained" relationships: relationships without full freedom or *true* love. We must never lose sight or erase from our memory the fact that our body is a temple of the Holy Spirit. "Do you not know that your body is a temple of the holy Spirit within you, whom you have from God? You are not your own …" [191] Therefore, let us take good care of our "temple." If through weakness or ignorance we have fallen,

---

[190] Genesis 1:27

[191] 1 Corinthians 6:19

it is never too late to start living a new life, pure and beautiful in the eyes of God. Let us run to confession,—and with a sincere purpose of amendment—change our life, and make of "our temple" the most beautiful and dignified … *God's favorite dwelling place!*

Another important factor to help a man choose the right spouse is to search for a pious woman who *shares his beliefs and religious traditions,* otherwise, the couple will be bringing *division* into their marriage from the very beginning. To be "one heart and one soul", we must share our faith because faith is lived within the soul. If a man practices a different religion than that of his future wife, they *cannot* be one heart: they are starting as two different, and maybe, very distant hearts! How can there be unity, if the greatest and most beautiful part of the couple is divided? "If a kingdom is divided against itself, that kingdom cannot stand." [192] If the Kingdom of God—which is found in the depths of our being (in our soul)—is *divided* against itself (because once married, man and woman become one flesh [193]), *it will not stand!* United since the beginning, the couple needs to search for the *Truth*. They need to *live* their faith and pray together *every day*. And because we love with our heart and soul, AS THE COUPLE GROWS IN THEIR LOVE FOR *GOD*, THEY WILL GROW IN THEIR LOVE FOR *EACH OTHER* TOO!

We need to plead to God *every* day for the person who will be our spouse and *avoid rushed decisions*. We must *not* feel frustrated if we have searched and have not found love; the person with whom we are willing to spend the *rest of our life* …

---

[192] Mark 3:24

[193] Genesis 2:24

We ought to pray daily for that person who awaits us somewhere—for the person that God has prepared for us from all eternity. But if the years pass by and we are still single, we must *not* despair. My brother wisely says: "the miserable unmarried man is happier than the miserable married man." If we don't find the person with whom we have full certainty that we will form a *holy, happy*, and *stable marriage* for the *rest* of our life—even if this sounds harsh—it is better not to marry! On the other hand, marrying because we think "this is our last chance" is as bad as not marrying for selfish reasons. Please, let us stop the craze of our times! No "sologamy"! We do not need to go to the court and wear a ring to live alone! Let us live simply. Let us place our life before God. Let us be open to His Most Holy Will, because only when we live according to God's Will we find our joy!

On the road of singleness, life is enriched and becomes more beautiful in the measure by which we give ourselves to the service of *God* and of *others*: to our family, community, parish, to the elderly, and to those who are most in need. If we are single, we can—and must—choose as the love of our life and as our eternal and ever faithful companions: God, and God's family (the Blessed Virgin Mary, the Saints, and every person—*without exception)*. The single person may choose to follow the example of Blessed Pier Giorgio Frassati, who was a young lay man that became a saint by dedicating his entire life to the service of God and of the Lord's souls ... There are so many people in need of love and understanding! We can *transform* and *give meaning to our life* if we strive to help, serve, and make *others* happy (beginning with our family). If in this loving service to others we search for God, we will certainly find Him—if we seek Him with all our heart, mind, and soul [194].

On the other hand, if a young man already has a girlfriend and realizes that there is something in her that he does not like, he needs to question himself objectively if this relationship is truly going to work as a marriage. The following questions might be helpful to recognize a courting that is "fixed on solid rock":

- Is *God* the First, the Center, and the most important Person in our relationship?
  Do we consider God's Will before we make our decisions—as a couple and/or individually?
- Do we have a prayerful spirit, a spirit of service, and of self-sacrifice?
  Do we pray together?
  Do we do little sacrifices together?
  Do we practice any acts of charity together?
- Is our relationship helping us to become better persons?
  Are we growing in our love for the Lord, for each other, and for others?
  Are we generous, kind, and respectful to every person?
  Are we practicing faith and virtue at a higher degree than before we started dating? How specifically?
- Is there a balance between faith and fun in our life together?
  Do we sacrifice what is important (our faith) to give more importance to what is not (fun or excessive work)?
  How, where, and to what activity do we dedicate more time?

---

[194] Deuteronomy 4,29

(The places and activities to which we dedicate more time are the most important—not as an idea, but proven by daily actions.)

- If an attractive person came to me, would I feel totally indifferent about it, or would doubts arise in my heart, making me wish that I was not dating?
  Do we "have eyes" only for each other—or now and then do we "look at the menu" (other good-looking people who pass by our side)?
  If I were 100% certain that I will find a better person in the future, would I consider breaking up this relationship? Am I convinced that, for me, there cannot be anyone better, because she is everything I ever wanted?
- Do I feel deeply happy when we are together?
  Are the moments in which I am with her the best moments of my life (independently of the activity that we are doing?)
  Does she really make me happy?
  Do I truly make her happy?
- Are we both willing to sacrifice to make the other happy?
  Is there one of us who always seems to give way, to make the other happy?
- Do I desire to spend my life serving her, without expecting anything in return? If that were to happen (that I live to serve her, and I very rarely receive anything in return), would I really live peacefully and joyfully for the rest of my life? Or will I become a miserable, bitter human being?
- Can we have nice, peaceful conversations—even

when there have been differences between us? Or is it "impossible" to talk when one of us is or has been angry? How do we solve our differences?

- Are we alike? Do we truly like the same things—or do I have to "adapt" just a "little bit"?
- Am I willing to protect my future family from every danger with heroism, sacrificing myself for their well-being? Will I always consider what is best for *them* first, leaving myself, my choices, and preferences behind?
  Does she feel safe and at peace when she is with me?
- Am I completely certain that my girlfriend is going to be a good wife, mother, companion, friend, and a good example for my children?
  Can I offer that I will be all the above to my wife and children, too?
- How will I be as a husband and father?
  Will I dedicate all my free time to my family?
  Will I actively seek to spend all the time I possibly can with them —by making a sincere effort—even to the point of leaving behind other activities, if this were necessary?
  Will I be looking forward to coming back home after a long, tiring workday—to spend time with my wife and children (to talk, play, and pray together)?
- Since I will be the head of my household, am I ready to make wise and prudent decisions?
  Does she support me and trusts in my decision-making skills?
  Does she admire me? Why or why not?
  Do I admire her? Why or why not?

Will I be able to live confidently, knowing that my wife's decisions will be wise and prudent?

- Are we open to having *all* the children that God wants to give us?
- Are we ready to take care, protect, help, guide, form, and educate our children in the faith and in the spiritual, moral, and human virtues?

  With God's help, are we seriously committed to teach these perennial, spiritual, and human virtues and values to our children, not only by our words, but above all by being a living example for them—an example that they can easily perceive and follow—by the coherence of our life?
- Will our children find in me a bright example of faith, love, and respect for God and His commandments?

  Will our children find in me a living example of love, care, and respect for their mom?

  Will our children find in my wife an example of faith, love, and respect for God and me?
- Am I a hard-working, responsible man?

  Will I be able to sustain our family?
- Am I willing to allow my wife to stay home—so that she takes care of our children while I go to work?

  Is she willing to stay home and sacrifice her own plans, career, and maybe many comforts, luxuries, vacations, trips, etc. (to take care and give the best: our constant love and care to our children)?
- Are we conscientious that, once married we will not be able to buy the same amount of clothes, shoes, etc., and that—to be

prudent—we might need to buy cheaper brands?

- Will we help each other with the household chores (whenever this is possible, when there is a special need, when we are sick or too tired)?
- Are we clean and orderly?
- Does she know how to cook—or will the kitchen be my exclusive "department"?
- Am I willing to welcome my future wife's family sincerely and lovingly?

  Is her family willing to love and welcome me?

  Is my fiancée willing to welcome my family sincerely and lovingly?

  Is my family willing to love and welcome my future wife?
- Should I really marry this person?

As a way of summary, we may ask the following question: Can we say that our *reality* with our fiancée or girlfriend is truly better than our *dreams*? "You know you're in love when you can't fall asleep because reality is finally better than your dreams" [195]. When a man is considering a commitment *for life*, it is very important for him to ponder if there are any particular aspects of his girlfriend's personality and life (past, present, and future, and the circumstances that surround her) with which he couldn't live for the rest of his life. It is very likely that these things will *not* change! We must not deceive ourselves. If there is anything that bothers us while we are dating or engaged, it will be even more annoying within marriage, and it will cause trouble! Consequently, the

---

[195] Doctor Seuss.

decision of getting married must be *seriously* considered by both. *Really seriously*. We both need to ponder if our relationship is making us better persons, more devout, humble, generous, kind, and joyful. We must earnestly question if we are *truly* meant for each other, and if we are willing to accept each other FOR LIFE *JUST AS WE ARE*, with our qualities and defects, with our family, work, and with everything that surrounds us "in sickness and in health." No matter how advanced we are into our relationship, if we realize that we are not meant for each other, for each other's benefit, we must have the courage to end the relationship, because *a broken engagement is better than a broken marriage!* Marriage is beautiful, but it is also "hard work." It is not wise to go into marriage thinking that everything is going to be always "perfect." This would be *dangerous* because marriage is between two human beings, and humans are not perfect. We must work to adjust to each other (even when there is great love between the spouses). As they say, "men are from Mars, women are from Venus." [196] This is why it is so important to try to know our future wife—and to allow her to know us—the best way possible. "The victory of truth is love." [197] Let us not "pretend" to be a different individual than the one we really are. Rather, let us live with *transparency* (without deception) so that the person who chooses us may know and love us just as we are—*before* committing to an engagement—because marriage IS FOREVER!

To test how well our fiancée knows us, we may ask ourselves: Does she know, see, and love me in the same way that

[196] Gray, John. *Men Are from Mars, Women are from Venus*. Harper Collins, 1992.

[197] Saint Augustine. Bishop of Hippo. Sermon No. 358,1.

God knows, sees, and loves me? If the answer is negative, we must delay our plans until we have brought into light those "dark" aspects of our past and present (of our personality, family, or work). We must "reveal" ourselves as we are, even when it is difficult, when it is scary to think that the relationship might end, once she knows what is now "veiled." We do not want the truth to come into light once we are married and end our union in divorce due to a lack of sincerity (before both of us decided to commit to each other for life). Let us be brave! It is much better to know if our fiancée is really in love with *us*, or with the person she *imagines* us to be! Also, because the man has been called by God to be the "head of his household," it is *essential* that the woman admires him. If she does, she will be always happy to follow him and will feel safe under his lead. For this same reason, the man must strive to be always wise, gentle, and prudent. Bring her flowers on unexpected occasions, tell her that you love her or that she looks beautiful (even when she is 80 years-old), bring her out for dinner or help her with the household chores, remind her how grateful you are for all she does at home and for the amazing way in which she takes care of your kids. Listen to her and make her happy by fulfilling her small requests (being faithful to a supermarket list, putting things in its proper place, etc.) Let us remember "a happy wife is a happy life".

Finally, the Lord might be calling us to be more fully dedicated to His service in the religious, consecrated, or priestly life. If this is the case, we must give a prompt response—and accept it with generosity, deep humility, gratitude, and joy—because it is the *greatest* gift that God can ever bestow upon a soul!

The call to a life fully surrendered to the Lord is a sublime gift, a marvelous gift. It is a very special election from *The Love* to love.

> *The fruit of this love is 'the election'... On the part of God, this election is the eternal desire to save man through a sharing in His own life in Christ ... The effect of this eternal gift, of this grace of man's election by God, is like a seed of holiness, or a spring, which rises in the soul as a gift from God Himself, who through grace gives life and holiness to those who are chosen.*[198]

God's calling must *never be feared* because when it comes it is accompanied by special graces that will help the generous man to fulfill this marvelous vocation. As stated before, God's calling must be *embraced* with deep love, humility, gratitude, and joy, "for many are called, but few are chosen." [199] The gift of the priesthood is most special because through a man—as an instrument—the Lord fulfills His promise to remain with us until the end of times. Also, through the priesthood, God provides the sinner with grace and salvation (in all the stages of life: from birth to death). If the priest lives the evangelical counsels (of poverty, chastity, and obedience) with purity, honesty, and integrity; if he practices *fidelity* to *Christ* and to *prayer* with a spirit of *sacrifice* and with

---

198 Pope Saint John Paul II, Encyclical Letter *Redemptoris Mater* – 1st Part: Mary in the Mystery of Christ, No. 1 Full of Grace. No. 8,4.

199 Matthew 22:14

true *love*, he "will become a better instrument of the power of the Holy Spirit to build up God's people into a holy dwelling-place for God." [200] What an amazing task this is: to save and sanctify God's Church! "Where there is a *holy* priest, there is a fervent parish; where there is a *fervent* priest, there is a good parish; where there is a *good* priest, there is a lukewarm parish, and where there is a *lukewarm* priest there is a cold parish." If the priest *loves* and *seeks God* in prayer and in his daily sacrifices, if he keeps his eyes fixed on Jesus, he will become a holy priest—the type of priest that the world needs so much!

> *In all your deeds and words, you should look upon Jesus as your model. Do so whether you are walking, keeping silence or speaking; whether you are alone or with others. He is perfect, and thus you will be not only irreprehensible, but praiseworthy.*[201]

Once a young man has given his whole life to the Lord—if he performs every action and pronounces every word with the Lord and for Him— whatever he does or says will fill him with the *greatest* and *highest* joy imaginable (even in the midst of sufferings). God will always be his Father and faithful Friend, his strength, his joy, his peace … and his all! If you have been called, please do not take any longer, surrender your life without measure to the love of

---

200 Address of St. Pope John Paul II to Clergy, Religious people and Laity. Bangkok, Thailand. May 11, 1984.

201 Saint Bonaventure, Doctor of the Church (1221-1274).

the Most Blessed Trinity, of His souls, and of His Church. You can be assured that you will find the *true happiness* here on earth and for all eternity. "Everyone who has left houses or brothers or sisters or father or mother or children or lands, for my name's sake, will receive a hundredfold, and inherit eternal life" [202].

B) *For married couples*. Since the couple has *freely* chosen and accepted each other in order for the two to be transformed into one—as it is God's Will—according to His words in the Gospel of Saint John "… that they may become perfectly one…" [203] and to achieve *the true happiness* in their marriage, it is very important to FORGET WHAT HAS BEEN LEFT BEHIND. "That is why a man leaves his father and mother and clings to his wife, and the two of them become one body." [204] This being "one body" goes far beyond the physical union: the spouses are called to be *one in God and one with God* (both of them are called to try to love like God, to think like Him, to see all things like the Lord sees them, and to feel like God feels about things)—with Him, for Him, in Him, *always!*

To fulfill the marriage covenant according to God's Plan, the spouses must constantly seek the Lord's help in PRAYER, because it is *only* through Divine aid that we can *be* and *live* as we ought. God is Love, the Creator and Giver of every good thing. *The closest we are to the Lord*, we become *more united* as a couple. His love and His goodness are so infinitely great that they " overflow," filling the spouses' hearts. A relationship lived *near God*

---

[202] Matthew 19:29

[203] John 17:23

[204] Genesis 2:24

is a holy, stable, and happy relationship. In contrast, the *farthest* we move away from Him, our relationship becomes colder, more superficial, and emptier. How long can a relationship like this last? I don't know, but surely not too long! Jesus said it, "He who abides in me, and I in him, he it is that bears much fruit, for *apart from me* you can do *nothing*."[205] Besides, the spouses who pray together form an almost indestructible "chain" because as Fr. Patrick Peyton used to say, "The family that prays together, stays together". Also, to live marriage *according to God's plan*, the spouses must try to be understanding, support each other, and even be willing to sacrifice any type of personal satisfaction—if this sacrifice were necessary, and if it would provide safety, joy, and peace to their spouse.

COMMUNICATION is vital for the couple. We must communicate with each other *always* and in a spirit of *humility:* with willingness to *listen* and to *recognize our own faults*. Similarly, we must know how to *remain silent*—if this were necessary—for the good of the relationship, for the betterment of our marriage, and for the unity of our family. If we have the endurance to wait for the proper time,—once we are ready to speak with prudence, patience, and charity—the Lord will bless us with beautiful graces of perseverance, unity, forgiveness, and true love. Let us remember that anger is *never* a good counselor, and that it can lead us to hurt the beloved. If we act in anger, we are in great peril of *gravely* damaging our marriage and the beauty of this sacred union—which has been consecrated to God.

---

[205] John 15:5

The spouses must love each other "even as Christ loved the church:" [206] giving our life for each other. "It is in the gift of oneself to the beloved that we discover and renew our own goodness, through the communion of persons; and where we learn the value of loving and of being loved … it is a love which respects and edifies the person …" [207] In our daily encounter, when at times weariness and differences arise, it is easy to lose sight of this calling to selfless love, manifested as a gift to the beloved. But *grace, humility, and true love* can suffice for our weakness. It is vitally important to remember that we are not alone when we accept the responsibilities imposed to us by marriage because we count on the ever near and ever faithful aid of the *Holy Ghost*. He is at our side and *on* our side, trying to help us achieve *true* love and unity in the faith and in the Lord. The Holy Father, Pope Benedict XVI, in his encounter with the families in Valencia, Spain, said,

> *If they [the spouses] remain open to the Spirit and implore His help, He will not fail to bestow on them the love of God the Father, made manifest and incarnate in Christ. The presence of the Spirit will help the spouses not to lose sight of the source and criterion of their love and self-giving, and to cooperate with Him to make it visible and incarnate in every aspect of their lives.* [208]

---

206 Ephesians 5:25

207 Human Sexuality: Truth and Meaning. Monsgr. Elio Sgreccia, Secretary. No. 9.

208 V World encounter with the families-City of Arts and Sciences- Sunday, July 9, 2006.

The best recipe to *grow* in love (as mentioned before) is *prayer*. When this prayer is united to OPENNESS TO LIFE, the couple reaches the *fullness of unity:* their union becomes a new being—a new person—who is the fruit and mirror of their mutual and total love and self-surrender to each other.

> *Marriage ... finds its full meaning in Christ. It is the sacrament in which a man and a woman make an exclusive and unbreakable gift of self to each other out of love. Through their faithful love they continue the work of the first creation, cooperating with God in the task of bringing new life into the world.* [209]

If for a ***GRAVE*** reason the couple needs to delay the coming of a new baby into their family, Holy Mother Church allows *Natural Family Planning* [210] (NFP). But the spouses need to be *very careful* and *honest* about their considerations. They must remember that one of the *main* reasons—if not the *most* important—for marriage, is *procreation.* In their mutual love and daily life, the spouses must constantly recall the beautiful blessings that are poured into their marriage when they are open to life and blessed with a new baby. Finally, the couple must recall the teachings of Holy Mother Church throughout the centuries:

---

[209] St. Pope John Paul II – Willemstad. May 13, 1990 – No. 4.

[210] https://www.magentayou.com – is an internet website in which you can find more information about natural family planning.

> *In the task of transmitting life, therefore, (husband and wife) are not free to proceed completely at will, as if they could determine in a wholly autonomous way the honest path to follow; but they must conform their activity to the creative intention of God, expressed in the very nature of marriage and of its acts, and manifested by the constant teaching of the Church.* [211]

Nowadays it is said: "Two hands = two children." Nevertheless, each hand has five fingers! Also, we take care of our children not only with our hands, but with our head and—above all—with our *heart*, and our heart has an infinite capacity! We must not fear receiving "too many" children into our home. They are the fruit of our love, but also the fruit of *God's* love, who is the Giver and Owner of *every* life. The couple will not have any *more* or any *less* children than the ones the Lord *allows* them to have if they are open to life. If your marriage is *blessed* with abundant children, thank God for this gift with deep humility! Appreciate it, treasure it, and share your marvelous experience wherever you go! You will not need to use words; your generous example suffices! Families which have been blessed by the Lord with numerous children are a *blessing* to our society and to the family itself because when a child grows up surrounded by siblings, he learns to be more generous and helpful. Children who are part of a big family will hardly ever feel lonely because when the youngest kid doesn't have any more siblings at home, he is already surrounded by the blessing of nieces

---

[211] His Holiness Paul VI – Humanae Vitae, 10.

and nephews with whom he can talk, share, and play!

If in His plans—sometimes mysterious—the Lord has not allowed you to have children of your own, you may also want to study the NFP. Natural Family Planning provides the necessary tools for the couple to know each other and to grow in love, sacrifice, and virtue. On some occasions, it has helped couples who couldn't conceive babies to be blessed with the gift of life. But, if in your efforts, you have not been able to achieve the pregnancy which you so much desired, please consider the possibility of *adoption.* Adoption is greatly beneficial for the adoptive parents, for the adopted children, and for the mother (or couple) in need of help—and with a prospect to finish the life of a small human being (for lack of monetary resources, for an unplanned pregnancy, or for any other circumstance out of their reach, or out of their possibilities). Adoption is greatly blessed by God, and it brings joy and unity to the new family. For the biological parents, for the adoptive parents, and for the little one —who is in danger of death—adoption offers stability and a future life in peace. Death will never be better for this little one than having a home. I hope we agree on this one!

On the other hand, doing *works of mercy* is another form of being "fruitful." It brings blessings and makes the couple grow in mutual love and in the *true happiness*. If the Lord has not blessed us with children, we can dedicate part of our free time to do works of charity—such as helping the needy or visiting the sick and the elderly (including our own parents). We can also pursue any other type of voluntary work that the Lord inspires us to or places on our path. Doing works of mercy together will give us great joy and fulfilment. It will unite us as a couple, and it will open the gates of Heaven for both!

C) To the families. The constant teaching of the Church has been that "The well-being of the individual person and of the human and Christian society is intimately linked with the prosperity of the marriage and family community." [212] It is the duty of each member of the household to do everything they can to become as similar to the Holy Family as possible. In a home like this, every member tries to fulfill their mission as faithfully as possible—for the well-being and uplifting of the others—by *always* seeking to *joyfully* love, respect, and serve.

a. *The parents.* We must always expect the arrival of our children with joy and as a gift and presence of God among us. Each child is a unique person—not just a body, but a *soul*—made in the image and likeness of *God*,[213] and *entrusted* to us so that we may help them "to know, love, and serve God and to be happy with Him, forever in Heaven." [214] We must not forget that this is our *first* and *most important* mission in life: to help those we love to get to *Heaven.*

> *The Christian family passes on the faith when parents teach their children to pray and when they pray with them; when they lead them to the*

---

[212] Gaudium et Spes No. 47.

[213] Genesis 1:26

[214] Baltimore Catechism. Fist Lesson: On the End of Man. Question #4.

> *sacraments and gradually introduce them to the life of the Church; when all join in reading the Bible, letting the light of faith shine on their family life and praising God as our Father.* [215]

Activities and hobbies are very good, but by far, the *best* thing that we can do for our children is to help them grow in their *love for God and for their neighbor.* If we teach our children when they are very little—I would say, when they are newborn—to talk to God with filial love, their love and friendship with the Lord will always be natural, "normal." They will know Jesus as their *Best Friend.* They will understand that they can always go to Him in their need, and that He will be always at their side. They will know that God listens to them and loves them because He is *Good* and *Faithful*. Every night—before going to bed—we must dedicate a few minutes to "talk to God," to thank Him for the gift of *life*, for the beautiful things that surround us, and for the many blessings that He gives us *daily*: for the gift of a family, for a ceiling over our head and a blanket to cover us, for food on our table for a kind gesture or a smile that we received during the day, for a new friend, for the little birds, the impressive mountains, the beautiful trees and flowers, etc. Let us tell Him how much we love Him, that we desire to be His best friend, to console His Sacred Heart, and to make Him happy. It is extremely important to remember *always* that

---

[215] His Holiness Benedict XVI - V World encounter with the families-City of Arts and Sciences- Sunday, July 9, 2006 (Cf. Familiaris Consortio Number 60).

> *The experience of being welcomed and loved by God and by our parents is the firm foundation, which always promotes the authentic growth and development of every man—so helpful to mature in the search for truth and love, and to move beyond ourselves to enter into communion with others and with God.*[216]

If our children know that they are loved by God and by us, they will be able to *mature* and to *conquer* life's trials.

As our children grow up, we must take time to sit down and *listen* to them. We need to look them in the eye while we are talking. Cellphones are forbidden in these moments which are dedicated exclusively to them! During our time together we can talk about what is important for our kids (even when it is not particularly important for us). When they ask, we must respond to all their questions with *patience*, without hastiness. We can use these conversations to continue inculcating in their hearts a great love and trust in God as their Father, as the best and most faithful Friend (who will always help them in their difficulties, challenges, and fears). Our children need us to speak *clearly, honestly,* and *simply* about the dangers of pride, the world, the flesh, the eyes, and the devil. We must show them the difference between what is pleasing to God and what offends Him. They *need* us to guide them!

---

[216] His Holiness Benedict XVI - V World encounter with the families-City of Arts and Sciences- Sunday, July 9, 2006.

The *difference* between good and evil—how important it is to help our children to see clearly that there *is* a difference! Kids need to know that their *good* actions will be *rewarded*, but their *bad* actions will always have a *temporal and eternal punishment.* How important it is to do so with so much firmness, but with so much love that they may learn to *do good, avoid evil,* and *obey* out of *conviction!* In this way, our children's relationship with God will be simpler, more caring, and filled with love. They will understand that if we love God, we must *keep His commandments*[217] and act according to *His* Will. Parents who—*in justice*—are *loving* and *firm* with their kids, *open* the way so that their children may know God as the Good Father He really is. Parents need to reflect *God's kindness, firmness,* and *justice* in the relationships with our children. We must help them understand that there is *always* an *authority above us,* whom we must obey with a spirit of *love.* Mom and dad have to teach the kids to form a *strong will-power* (accepting, embracing, and seeking sacrifice in the *small* things of our *daily* lives and duties). If our children *obey* from the earliest years, as adolescents and adults they will welcome God's Will in their lives out of love and conviction (not only out of fear). Most importantly, they will experience the joy of knowing that they are loved by the Best of all fathers!

There is no "pattern" with which we can educate our children; each human being is special, unique, and—consequently— each one will understand and embrace grace in a different way, at a different time, and through diverse paths. Aided by Divine grace, we must pray to God that we may understand

---

[217] John 14:15

which is the specific path through which we must guide *each* of our children. Equally important is to patiently *wait* for them. If our kids are not "ready" (in a good disposition) to listen to us when we speak about God, we need to "speak to God about our children." While the *Lord's* moment comes (that precious moment in which *He* will touch their hearts with His grace and truth)—out of true love for them and by obedience to God—we must *correct* them when their actions are *separating* them from the Lord and from the path of righteousness. This is *the reason* for which God entrusted us with our children. As we heard in a previous chapter, according to Sacred Scripture, "… the Lord disciplines him whom He loves …" [218] If we love our children, following the example of the Best of all fathers, we must "re-direct" them when they are not on the right path.

Let us also consider that tomorrow's world depends on the way in which we form and help our children *today* (or when God gives them to us and entrusts them to our care). Whether we have been blessed with the gift of children—or not yet—we must *pray daily* for the gift of the HOLY GHOST for our kids (or our future kids). We need to ask the Father that our children may understand and accept—with joy and confidence—the Sanctifier's loving guidance. And we also need to ask the Lord for this most precious Gift (the Sanctifier—the Giver of wisdom, counsel, and understanding) for ourselves. *Only* under the guidance of the Holy Ghost we will be able to lead our kids with wisdom and prudence through the path that will bring them to Heaven.

---

[218] Letter to the Hebrews 12:6

We need to pray daily for the *graces* that our children *need* to be holy and to be willing to joyfully *surrender* their lives to God (wherever they are and whatever they do). As parents, we need to beg God that they may—simply and clearly— understand where and how to serve the Lord *better*, according to *His* Will and to the *qualities* He has given them. We must implore the Giver of every good thing that each one of our children may fulfill the Divine Plan with fidelity, sincerity, and love. Our most earnest prayer should be that they may always be holy, generous, and faithful. If their path is the married life, we can offer our prayers so that the Lord help them to become the best husband/father or wife/mother. And let us not forget to implore graces of holiness also for their *future spouse*. It is very important to keep in our prayers our children's *friends* and *all* the people who surround them. *Only* God—in His infinite mercy—can *free* them from harmful people, activities, and influences.

Let us take care of what our children *see* and *hear*. Our brain is a computer that "stores" all the information that comes through our senses and brings it out when we least expect it. The "input" makes us react and think in unexpected ways, and—especially when the input has been the *wrong* one—our thoughts, words, and actions become inappropriate.

A marvelous "remedy" to help our children in their fight against evil is to pray the Holy Rosary for them. When they are little and in need of much attention, we can pray at least one Rosary a day for all our kids and offer up our work throughout the day for them. As they grow up—and if we have more free time—we must do everything possible to pray one Rosary a day for *each* one of our sons and daughters. If Our Lord has blessed us with many children, we can offer up as many daily Rosaries as we *can* (if we are able to pray only one, let us pray one, but let us pray it *fervently*: with all our heart, reverence, and attention). If we have any "free seconds" during the day, we can offer Hail Mary's to the Queen of the Universe and Mother of God, so that *She* may take care of our kids and guide them through the path that leads them to Heaven. We must entrust the sanctification of our children and place each one of them in the Heart of the Most Blessed Trinity, the Blessed Virgin Mary, and dearest Saint Joseph—begging Them to make them grow as true children of God, as "new creatures" who will give glory to God in their words, thoughts, and actions. Let us not forget to beg the Holy Ghost *daily* to fill the minds and hearts of our kids with His seven gifts and twelve fruits. Jesus said that the Father would give the Holy Spirit to those who pray for this most necessary Gift [219]. Let us pray for it! Finally, if possible, we should make an effort to offer at least one hour of weekly Eucharistic adoration before the Blessed Sacrament for our family. If we have an adoration chapel near us, we must thank the Lord for this most precious gift. If we don't, we can always visit the Most Blessed Trinity for an hour, in any church—where the Lord is alive, present, and waiting for us in the Tabernacle. Maybe a good moment to do this could be on our date night. Parents, we must be devout!

The parents' example is very important, but the *father's* example is *exceptionally* fundamental! The father's *virtue* will be reflected in the children's *virtue*. The father's *vice* will be reflected in the children's *vice*. The father's faith will be reflected in his

[219] Luke 11:13.

children's faith and in their physical, spiritual, and mental well-being. If the father goes to Mass on Sundays, the children will go to Mass (even when they are older and away from home). If the father does *not* go to Mass—even when the mother is a daily communicant—the kids will *not* go. If the father is charitable and generous, the kids will follow. If the dad criticizes and is selfish, that is the way his children will turn out to be. If the father sins—even when he is alone and nobody else, but God, sees him—the children will sin in the same way! If the father remains always near, understanding, and affectionate towards his children, if he spends time with them, boys and girls alike will grow physically, emotionally, and spiritually *strong*.

As the popular saying goes: "Actions speak louder than words." Saint Francis of Assisi told his spiritual children "Preach the Gospel at all times, and if necessary, use words." We must offer a *good example* to our children by living a pure, coherent, and generous life. We must *pray together* and do *works of mercy* with them; this will facilitate our children to understand the Gospel as a living reality. We must try our best to be the *good parents* the *Lord* wants us to be, but we need to keep in mind that God *alone* can enlighten and ennoble the most difficult and beautiful work and responsibility that a human being can receive: the raising and formation of children!

Briefly, and as a summary of all the above, some very *practical* aspects of family life:

- *Helping our children to enjoy doing chores around the house.* Even if we don't need help, we must allow them to sweep, dust, wash clothes and dishes, clean bathrooms, cook, etc. By doing all these activities, our children will learn to be humble, helpful and respectful; they will learn to appreciate the people who do these types of activities for them.

- *Keeping a bedtime schedule and routine.* This will give stability to the kids.
- *Teaching them the "magic words"* (please, thank you, and sorry) —from the moment they start talking. It is never too early for this!
- *Not using the television or electronic devices as "baby-sitters."* It is so much healthier for our kids to read, play, do puzzles, run, bike ride, walk at the park, etc.
- *Taking our kids on hikes, camping, or trips.* This unites the family and provides the children with skills and knowledge that cannot be received in a classroom.
- *Playing with our children.* Taking time to play with our kids is very significant: we show them our love, closeness, and attention. They know they are important! Nevertheless, when we play with them, we must not let them always win—It will help them understand that in life, sometimes we win and sometimes we lose.
- *Helping our children create the habit of tidying up*—their room and after they have finished playing.
- *Not giving our kids everything they want* (especially, if they throw a temper tantrum to get it). This way they will appreciate their things more, and will have something to look forward to—particularly if it was difficult for them to obtain. They will also learn that we cannot always have what we want;

that it is easier to obtain what we want when we work hard and when we ask nicely than when we demand or cry; that most times, we need to wait for a while before we can acquire good things.

- *Not giving our kids a cell phone until they are mature enough* (Maybe after they are 15 years-old—and if we can wait even longer—we must do it!). This will preserve them from many temptations and probably sins; contrary to what people may believe, it will also keep them *more* sociable because children who have a cell phone tend to become isolated!
- *Conversing with our children* (beginning when they are small); but also, teaching them that it is important to have moments dedicated to *silence, prayer,* and *work.*
- *Not expecting our kids to know everything already.* We must teach them how to behave in every circumstance—and before the moment arises. For example, if we will be going to Mass, we need to tell them (at their own level) that we will be going to see Jesus; that He deserves all our love, respect, and attention. We must clarify also everything that we are expecting from them during that specific time. Another example, if it is time to go to the supermarket, we must let them know that we will go shopping and that they should not ask for anything because we will not be able to buy it for them. This way the kid is under advice, and he will understand what the right behavior is—what he can and *cannot* do! [220] If our children still do not comply with what we taught them, we do not need to get frustrated and start yelling. We must remember that they are

[220] Wise advise from Doctor Edward Sri.

learning. We can just say "remember what we talked about…" When we get back home, we will be in a better condition to sit with them and *calmly* talk about their behavior. We must try to help them reflect and understand if their actions were right or wrong and *why*.

- *Not screaming or insulting our children while we are correcting them.* If we do so, they will automatically close their senses to our words. Our kids will not listen to us! Let us remember Saint Theresa's words: "Patience achieves *ALL* things." Our patience and love can achieve much more than *all* our yelling!
- *Never giving a punishment to our kids while we are upset or angry.*
- *Making sure that our punishments are for a just cause, and reminding our children that we are doing it because we love them* and because we want them to be *better people*. It is very important to give them *reasonable* punishments (neither too much, nor too long, nor too severe.)
- *Dialoguing, reasoning, and accepting our own mistakes, and solving the differences in love*. This will bring great happiness and peace to our home.
- *Helping our children know and understand that, at home, mom and dad are the authority*—not out of tyranny—but because it is *God's Will*. There will always be someone above us whom we must obey (on Earth and in Heaven). It is highly important for the little ones to understand this fact from their most tender infancy.
- *Never disagreeing with our spouse in front of the children.* Arguing (especially if there is yelling involved) is more harmful

for the couple—and for the kids—than the problem itself.

- *Informing our children (since they are little) about the dangers of drugs,* and as they grow up, explaining to them the *terrible effects and consequences of the sins against the sixth and ninth commandments*. It is not necessary to be "graphic." An honest, simple, childlike explanation, can have a lasting effect in their mind and heart—especially if our children trust us. In most cases, we can't wait too long before talking about these things with them. It might be too late! We don't want someone else to introduce them to these topics …
- *Inviting our children's friends to our home and praying for those friends—and for their future friends*. Friends have a powerful influence on our kids and on their behavior and choices.
- *Praying for our daughters' boyfriends and sons' girlfriends and welcoming them as part of our family.*
- *Teaching our children to be generous and share*—especially the things they like most! If our kids are generous with others, they will be generous with God, and they will have a better opportunity to achieve a greater degree of holiness.
- *If we wish our children to speak always well of others ... We must begin with our own example!*
- *Most importantly, we must nurture in our children a great love of God:*

**Present in others*. "If anyone says, 'I love God,' and hates his brother, he is a liar; for he who does not love his brother whom he has seen, cannot love God whom he has *not* seen." [221] We ought

[221] 1 John 4:20

to help our kids to understand this reality. We should not let them criticize or hurt anyone (physically or morally). Rather, we must nurture positive conversations and appreciation for people and their qualities. To achieve this, it may be helpful to bring our kids to give toys to the poor and food to the hungry, take them to visit the elderly … or accompany them to do any other work of mercy that comes to mind or that we prefer.

**Through the interior life.* It is very important to place a small altar at home and to pray the Holy Rosary with our children *every* day. Other ways in which we can foster the interior life of our kids are: to make a brief examination of conscience, give thanks, ask for forgiveness, and bless them every night before bedtime. Let us also bless the food—with which the Lord has so generously provided our family—before every meal, and give thanks when we are finished. The most important activity of the whole week is going to Mass every Sunday and dedicating the day to the Lord and to the family. If we are able to go to daily Mass, we must take advantage of this opportunity. There is no better gift than this! Holy Week is the holiest time of the year. Let us make it *holy!* Let us participate in the Sacred Triduum, offer up sacrifices and fasts with joy and generosity … and please, let us leave vacations for *another* time during the year. Another way in which we can keep the faith of our children alive is participating in the processions offered by the Church—through different parishes—especially on the Feast of Corpus Christi. We can also make pilgrimages to different sanctuaries (if our budget does not allow the family to travel far, we can go, at least, to the nearest city). An idea to foster love for Our Lady in our children is to honor Her, especially during the month of

May by having our children collect some wild flowers, buy a small bouquet, or draw flowers for Mary, and bring them to Her (either to our home altar or to the Church) once a week. When we do so, we can ask Our Lady to always be our Mother, thank Her for Her love and protection, and entrust our family to Her loving care. These are only a few ideas. May the Holy Ghost be our guide in every effort we make to help our kids grow in the interior life!

- *Reading to our children.* Reading offers a marvelous opportunity for the family to share time, be near, and have nice conversations. There are many books, but the *best* reading we can offer them is the Bible—primarily the New Testament—because in it we find the treasure of the life and words of Jesus and His Apostles. The reading of the *lives of the saints* will also fill the minds and hearts of our children with exemplary teachings.
- *Helping our children form a strong willpower.* The best way to do this is through *little daily sacrifices*: doing what is difficult for us with a smile and without complaining; eating a little of the things we do not like, and not eating what we like; waiting a few extra minutes before eating (when we are already feeling "starved"); doing homework responsibly and to the best of one's abilities; standing and sitting up straight, etc.
- *Loving the Blessed Virgin Mary and trusting in Her powerful intercession.* Helping our children to have a tender love for Our Lady beginning when they are little will result in a big difference in their lives because She is the *best* Mother, the *best* Protection against the devil and against every one of life's dangers.

- *Loving, knowing, and living our faith.* This is the best way in which we can transmit it to our kids and it is also the best "inheritance" we can leave them.
- *Seeking holiness.* If the father is near God, the children will follow. If the father is distant from God, his children will also be separated from God and from His commandments.

Unquestionably, the first to be held accountable for the family's flourishment as a community of love, peace, and joy are the parents.

> *Christian married couples and parents, following their own path, should support one another in grace all through life with a faithful love and should educate their children—lovingly received from God—in the Christian doctrine and in the evangelical values. In this way they present to all an example of unfailing and generous love…*[222]

Only God can help us with this, which is the greatest and most important of all missions: the mission to make our family a home full of peace, love, understanding, and unselfish surrender to the Lord and to each other.

b. *The children.* Parents await their children with deep love. Each child is a gift for them. In His infinite wisdom, God joins the members of each family with Divine bonds. No child has ever

---

[222] Lumen Gentium, 41.

chosen his parents' qualities or temper, nor have the parents ever chosen their children's qualities or temper. God created us from the union of our father and mother, and *He* has given them to us as the gift to show us the path that better leads us to His Will. Whoever obeys his parents—in all those things that are moral and according to the Gospel's teachings—by God's mysterious design, obeys the Lord Himself. As Saint Paul reminds us, "Children, obey your parents in the Lord, for this is right."[223]

It is remarkable that after the three first commandments—which refer to our relationship with God Himself—the fourth one refers to our relationship with our parents: "Honor your father and your mother." As the years go by, some children tend to think that they "know better." They (we) forget that once mom and dad were young too. They—most likely— were exposed to the same situations that we are living at this moment, and they speak to us with "the voice of experience," but above all, with a heart full of *great* and *unconditional* love. Other times, we forget that the desire to protect us from sufferings, difficulties, and anxieties is in our parents' nature. Because it is God's Will, if we truly want *to grow, mature, and achieve the true happiness*, we must listen to our parents and take their advice. They count on Divine graces to aid us. Nobody will ever love us as our parents do! Nobody desires our wellbeing, prosperity, and eternal salvation like them. If for some reason we don't agree with their advice, we can always express our opinion—with love and respect—and together conclude what is best for us. Let us remember Saint Augustine's example, who for many years despised his mother's advice and care. Persevering, she

---

223 Ephesians 6:1

prayed unceasingly for him. Augustine was baptized when he was 33 years-old; nine years later he became a Bishop, and today he is a Saint and Doctor of the Church!

On the other hand, it is necessary to remember that some elderly people might become a little "stubborn." As the years go by, we may become "children" again. We do not like to be alone, and we need to be looked after. Our health, memory, sight, and hearing begin to fail. How unfair it would be to forget all those years in which our parents looked after us! They fed us, changed us, cleaned us, and "put up" with us. Let us be charitable and fill them with love, understanding, support, and service. Our parents have devoted their entire life to us; they have given us their love and support through the years. "Kindness to a father will not be forgotten, and against your sins it will be credited to you … In the day of your affliction, it will be remembered in your favor; as frost in fair weather, your sins will melt away" [224].

Finally, let us allow Pope John Paul II's cry to resound deep in our hearts: "The future of humanity is forged in the family!" [225] Families, let us forge the kind of humanity that God dreamed of when He created us: a more devout, Christian, united, faithful, kinder, a more generous—in giving and forgiving—, a humbler, simpler, and a happier humanity!

The specific mission of the family is to embody love and to put it at the service of society: conjugal love, paternal and maternal love, fraternal love, the love

---

224 Sirach 3:14-15

225 Homily in Willemstad (Dutch Antilles)-Sunday, May 13, 1990-No.5.

> *of a community of persons and generations, love lived under the sign of a couple's faithfulness and fecundity for a civilization of love and of life.* [226]

Dear Lord, please touch our lives and our homes with Your Spirit of Truth and Love so that each member of our family may be a reflection of *Your* love in the kindness and service we offer each other and our neighbor. We ask this, through Jesus Christ, Your Beloved Son, Our Lord. Amen.

[226] The Eucharist, gift of God for the Life of the World-Theological document used for the Eucharistic International Congress in Quebec- July 30, 2006 - VI – Witnesses of the Eucharist in the Heart of the World –B. The family, the domestic Church, foundation of a civilization of love.

CHAPTER XI: An Exceptional Beauty

Most people I know worry about external appearances: wrinkles, hair loss, the "extra" pounds, a most perfect and whiter smile, etc. For this reason, it is important to dedicate a few lines to the most beautiful and radiant super-model of this century. This super-model wasn't even 5 feet tall, she had a noticeable hump, and her face was "a grid" of wrinkles. Her name: Mother Teresa of Calcutta.

God granted me the grace of meeting her for a few minutes, and I can truly say that she is the most beautiful woman I have ever seen! All her being *reflected God:* her little bright eyes, her smile, and her tears; the strength of her handshake; the sincerity of her surrender at the service of God and the "poorest of the poor" and the greatness of her love … What an exceptionally beautiful woman!

We must always try to be clean and well arrayed to give glory to our Creator, and also as a reflection of the dignity we bear as children of God, but our *true* efforts—and our *higher* aspirations—must be to reach the *only* beauty that can lead us to a personal encounter with God, who is the *true happiness.*

> *The desire for God is written in the human heart, because every person has been created by God and for God; and God never ceases to draw man to Himself, and only in God will he find the truth and happiness he never stops searching for.* [227]

[227] Catechism of the Catholic Church No. 27.

If we really want to be "radiant" like Mother Teresa, we must not worry about our external appearances, but about our most intimate being: the place where our soul meets with God. Can we achieve this beauty that goes far beyond all telling and all physical appearances?

A) *Interior life*. The interior life of a person begins with his openness to faith. "Faith is to believe what you do *not* see; the reward of this faith is *to see* what you believe."[228] Since faith is a theological virtue, it will come into our hearts as a gift from God's love through baptism. When our faith is not strong enough, we must *pray* for this gift and take *good care* of it once we have received it. To obtain, preserve, and increase our faith, it is useful to do frequent *acts* of faith and love: "I believe; help my unbelief!"[229] "Lord, I know that You are here with me. I know that You love me, that You take care of me, that You listen to me, that You see me, that You protect me, that You want the best for me." "Lord, You are All-powerful; there is nothing impossible for You." "Lord, help me! I believe in You" …

God desires to give us the gift of faith *superabundantly.* He is always at our side, but He wants us to seek Him and to "knock at the doors" of His Most Sacred Heart: "Ask, and it will be given you; seek, and you will find; knock, and it will be opened to you."[230] We can "knock" with a *humble* prayer which recognizes our insignificance, indignity, and our *need* to remain united to the Vine. Faith and humble prayer help us to remember that to bear fruit we

228 Saint Augustine, Bishop of Hippo. Doctor of the Church.

229 Mark 9:23

230 Matthew 7:7-8

need to remain united to the Lord because without Him we can do *nothing!* [231]

The beauty, peace, and love of God can *only* be reflected by a person who possesses a deep *interior* life. These virtues are the fruit of the Lord's presence in the soul who sincerely seeks Him. Without the Lord, without His grace, it is *impossible* to attain virtue. Accordingly, we must take very seriously our commitment of friendship with the Most Blessed Trinity. We call our friends, we visit them, and we honestly demonstrate our affection by trying to do what pleases them … And, what pleases the Friend of our soul? How can we show Him that we really love Him?

If we love God, it is necessary to consider that the greatest gift we can offer Him is our *will* (totally surrendered to *His* Most Holy Will out of love). The Good Lord knows it and highly values this gift! When a person *surrenders* his will to God and *sincerely* tries to fulfill His commandments, the Lord listens to his prayers and grants the petitions requested by the faithful soul—when these are not opposed to the salvation of his soul or the salvation of the soul of others. Everything that God *gives* us, or what He *does not*, is for *our good*. This must be the certitude and hope that help us to welcome—and embrace—*His* most Holy Will as *ours*.

Another way to show the Lord that we truly love Him, is to keep His word. "Whoever loves me will *keep* my word, and my Father will love him, and we will come to him and make our dwelling with him." [232] The following are suggestions to help us know and *keep* His Word:

---

[231] John 15:5
[232] John 14:23

a. *Invoking the Holy Ghost.* The Holy Spirit is the Faithful Friend of our souls, the Sanctifier, the Advocate. He guides us to the full truth [233]—in other words—He guides us through the straight path towards *Jesus*, who is *the* Truth. "Nobody is able to say, 'Jesus is Lord' except in the Holy Spirit." [234] Let us ask Him to speak in us and for us. Let us pray that the Paraclete may open the eyes of our soul to contemplate—in all its grandeur—God's beauty and kindness. Let us ask the Holy Ghost for the gift of remaining firmly and faithfully adhered to Him in love. Let us also beg the Holy Ghost to seal—with the fire of His love—our mind, intelligence, and will; our words and actions; our affections, our heart, and our whole life. May each and every one of our thoughts, words, and actions—inspired and moved by Him—always glorify the Father and seek the well-being of our brethren.

b. *Visiting Jesus in the Eucharist.*

> *Here on earth, it's impossible to perform a more meritorious act than visiting Jesus often in the Eucharist. If you took all the good works done by all the humans who have ever lived in all of history and stacked them all up and multiplied them by a million, they wouldn't equal the merit, virtue, and worth of one Mass. The Eucharistic sacrifice is Christ's infinite merit and worth.* [235]

---

233 John 16:7-13

234 1 Corinthians 12:3

235 Saint Teresa of Avila, Doctor of the Church.

As mentioned before, Jesus is *truly* present in the Holy Eucharist. Even when He is *humbly hidden* in that small piece of bread, HIS PRESENCE IS *REAL*. He is always silently and patiently awaiting us because He desires to fill our souls with His grace and love. Let us not leave Him waiting! Let us go to Eucharistic adoration, go to Holy Mass, and receive the Lord in Holy Communion as frequently, fervently, and faithfully as we can.

> *When you have received Him, stir up your heart to do Him homage; speak with Him about your spiritual life, gazing upon Him in your soul, where He is present for your happiness; Welcome Him as warmly as possible, and behave outwardly in such a way, that your actions may give proof to all, of His Presence.*[236]

In this "common-union," the infinite God and our nothingness are fused together in the most perfect way. When communion is received *worthily*, the Lord fulfills His work of *transformation* in our souls. Little by little, our being becomes one in Him, with Him, and by Him … What a marvelous gift awaits us in the Holy Eucharist! Let us not despise Him!

c. *Praying*. "Those who pray the most will be saved, those who pray little are in great danger, and those who do not pray are lost."[237] According to the Baltimore Catechism,

---

236 Saint Francis de Sales (1567-1622). Doctor of the Church

237 Saint Padre Pio of Pietrelcina.

> *Prayer is the lifting up of our minds and hearts to God to adore Him, to thank Him for His benefits, to ask His forgiveness, and to beg of Him all the graces we need whether for soul or body*[238].

It is said about the late Pope Saint John Paul II that one day while he was in prayer, someone came to interrupt him:

> —"Holy Father, I'm sorry to bother you, but this is really important …"

The Holy Father answered, "Is it very important?"

> — "Yes, Holy Father!"
>
> — "Then … Let us continue praying!"

… God can solve *any* conflict, even those which seem enormous and super-complicated. We must come to Him *frequently* and *constantly*, full of confidence and humility. "God, grant me the serenity to accept the things I cannot change, courage to change the things I can, and wisdom to know the difference." [239] Justice, peace, and *every good thing* come from the Lord. We must not be anxious about the things we cannot solve; let us simply pray, trusting in His infinite love, power, and mercy. "For me, prayer is an impulse of the heart, a simple gaze at Heaven, a cry of gratitude and love in sorrow as in joy." [240] It is extremely important to approach the Lord as our best Friend and seek Him *always*, not only when we are in need … the Lord is not an *aspirin!* We must *constantly* draw close

---

238 The Baltimore Catechism – Second part: On Prayer – No. 304.

239 Richard Niebuhr, "The Serenity Prayer".

240 St. Teresa of Avila. Doctor of the Church.

to God especially to praise and thank Him. The fruits of prayer are incredible: prayer strengthens our faith, nourishes our hope, increases our love for God, keeps us humble, merits grace, and atones for sin [241]. Prayer is a means to establish communication with God. It is a privileged time to encounter Our Creator and Our *All*.

We have the possibility to do mental prayer and vocal prayer, but we must not forget Jesus' words, "And in praying do not heap up empty phrases as the gentiles do; for they think that they will be heard for their many words."[242] We do not need to talk unceasingly to be heard: our work and efforts, every instant, and our whole life can become a prayer—and even contemplation—when we keep the Lord always in our thoughts and in our heart. As Saint Teresa of Avila said, "Jesus walks amidst the pots and pans." Whatever our duties may be—the laborious and difficult enterprises or simply to cook, sweep, clean, write, study, plan, or any other occupation—they are privileged places and moments in which we can also unite our soul to the Lord in prayer (as long as we *offer up* our simple work with sincere effort and love).

There are several moments and forms of prayer: Holy Mass, adoration of the Blessed Sacrament, the Holy Rosary, the Divine Office, the Way of the Cross, the Chaplet of Divine Mercy, novenas, etc. Regardless of the type of prayer we choose to say, we must avoid the "empty words." May our words come out from our heart—not from our lips—so that Jesus will not have to reproach us, "This people honor me with their lips, but their hearts are far

---

241 The Baltimore Catechism–Third Part: On Prayer–No. 1117.

242 Matthew 6:7

from me"[243].

Being talkative is God's marvelous gift, but equally important is to keep silence and listen. The Lord needs our *silence* to communicate with our soul. Let us keep in mind that "God has given us two ears and one mouth, because we need to *listen* more and to talk *less*".

To prepare our soul for our personal encounter with the Lord—especially when we pray in Church, in front of the Blessed Sacrament, or after communion—it is greatly beneficial to remember that we are in the Presence of *God,* who is Omnipotent and Eternal. If it is helpful, we can picture the Lord seating on His Throne surrounded by hundreds of angels who constantly adore Him. We can ask Him to place us beside them, so that the angels—especially our Guardian Angel—may help and teach us to pray with them, and as them: with profound love, adoration, fervor, and gratitude for the gift of our creation and for being able to serve Him; for the opportunity to remain in His Presence this day and for all eternity (as long as we try to fulfill His commandments and to live in grace). We can also ask the Lord for the gift to adore Him like the angels, in an attitude of awe, admiration, humility, and reverence before His greatness and majesty. Nevertheless, maybe the most important thing to be well prepared for prayer is to remember Saint Teresa of Avila's words: "To pray is to talk about *love* with *Him,* whom as we know *loves us*".

If a person wishes to know if his time of prayer was a *true* encounter with the Lord, he may ask himself—once he is

[243] Mark 7:6

finished praying—if his heart is burning in love for God; if he has an increased desire for holiness; if he has a better comprehension of his misery and of the Lord's Mercy, and a better understanding of a mystery or a truth of our faith— and has accepted it more fully; finally, he can analyze if he has come out of prayer with great peace and with a firm resolution to do good and to avoid evil. All of these are good indicators that this person has, indeed, spent time with the Lord!

Gustave Flaubert [244] said: "If we would always look towards Heaven, we would end up having wings." May our prayer be so beautiful, deep, and real, that it may give us the *wings* we need to fly up to God and to find in Him the *true happiness!*

d. *Keeping silent.* The first "wings" we need—if we wish to obtain from God the gift of this beautiful, deep, and transforming prayer—is *silence*. "There is no need of wings to go in search of God, but to seek *solitude*, and to look for Him *within* oneself." [245] Have you ever tried to keep a conversation with someone at a night club? It is almost impossible! Likewise, to be able to sustain a conversation with God, we need a "favorable atmosphere": an ambience of recollection, solitude, and silence. The Lord's *soft* voice[246] can only be heard in the *silence* of our soul. We live in a "mad" world, totally crazy! We run from place to place, doing things and more things. We get in the car and turn on the radio; we go everywhere with the cell phone at hand; we get home and turn on the TV. If

---

244 French novelist, considered one of the greatest exponents of Literary Realism.

245 Saint Teresa of Avila. Doctor of the Church.

246 1 Kings 19:11-13

we dedicate a little bit of time to prayer, we spend those minutes looking at our watch. … Do we seriously think that, like this, we will be able to hear, know, and love God? God is a Friend, God is Love, God is Faithful, God is Good! Why does it seem so difficult for us to give a little bit of time to someone as *amazing* as Him? Could the answer be that we do not know the Lord, mainly because we are used to living by the *senses?* Our Lord needs us to give Him *His* own space, time, and place. "When you pray, go to your inner room, close the door, and pray to your Father in secret. And your Father who sees in secret will repay you."[247] God's reward for those who search for Him (even when they don't see or hear Him) is far beyond anything imaginable: *knowledge and love of God* are the *greatest* treasure, the "fine pearl"[248] of incomparable value!

Besides giving God His place and time—above all—we must give Him our *heart*. Since God is faithful, He will reward our efforts, placing us very near *His* own Heart. Living in God's Heart! There cannot be—in this life or in Heaven—a *greater* and *more profound joy* than this!

e. *Opening the Gospels.* According to Saint Jerome, "Ignorance of Scripture is ignorance of Christ." When we read Matthew, Mark, Luke, and John, we are walking the roads of Galilee, Samaria, and Judea alongside Jesus—and we are being held by His hand. At these moments, we need to look at Him, listen to Him, and meditate on His words with attention and with an open heart. He will talk to us in a personal way and with perfect clarity, but we

---

247 Matthew 6:6.

248 Matthew 13:45-46.

need to be careful *not* to fall into the trap of expecting to hear the Lord with our physical ears. Let us remember that we must *listen* to God in the *silence* of prayer and contemplation—but also—in the advice, example, and wisdom of others, in our personal experiences, and in the events that we have witnessed throughout our life.

f. *Fulfilling the commandments.* "If you love me, you will keep my commandments." [249] God loves us, and He wants us to be with Him in Heaven. His love is so pure and so great that He showed us the way to follow (so that we don't have to keep guessing how to get there). The instructions are crystal clear, easy to understand for all: the commandments.

"He who has my commandments and keeps them, he it is who loves me." [250] The commandments—contrary to what many people might think—are not "heavy burdens," "rigid" rules, "impossible impositions"; but rather, a *love path.* On one hand, they are a manifestation of *God's love for men*, a safe guide to get to Heaven and to obtain *freedom and true happiness.*

> *If you obey the commandments of the Lord your God which I command you this day, by loving the Lord your God, by walking in his ways, and by keeping his commandments and his statutes and his ordinances, then you shall live and multiply …*[251]

---

[249] John 14:15

[250] John 14,21

[251] Deuteronomy 30:16

And, on the other hand, fulfilling the commandments is a manifestation of *men's love and respect for God*. According to Jesus' words,

> *You shall love the Lord your God with all your heart, and with all your soul, and with all your mind. This is the great and first commandment. And a second is like it, you shall love your neighbor as yourself. On these two commandments depend all the law and the prophets.*[252]

Whoever loves God and others, automatically fulfills *all* the commandments. One who loves neither kills, nor steals or deceives.

> *... He who loves his neighbor has fulfilled the law. The commandments 'You shall not commit adultery, you shall not kill, you shall not steal, you shall not covet,' and any other commandment, are summed up in this sentence, 'You shall love your neighbor as yourself.' Love does no wrong to a neighbor; therefore, love is the fulfilment of the law.* [253]

A person who truly loves, naturally fulfills all the commandments.

---

252 Matthew 22:37-40

253 Romans 13:8-10

B) *Not fearing sacrifice*. A person who denies himself—to seek the wellbeing of others, to serve them and to make them happy—becomes a living image of God: The Father offered *with* and *in* His Beloved Son the *ultimate* sacrifice so that we could be saved. Whoever is detached from himself also becomes a "mirror" of Jesus—who offered up even the last drop of His blood so that we could be washed in it and obtain eternal life.

Each one of us knows within ourselves which are the sacrifices that we can offer up to help others. At times, our sacrifice will be to give up what we like or desire (activities, food, pastimes, rest) if this can allow someone else to have it, if it gives them rest, or if it offers them peace and joy. Maybe our sacrifice will entail *not* performing a sacrifice that we really longed for (in the depths of our soul) because obedience commands us not to do so. Other times, our sacrifice will be transformed in giving what we have, whom we love, or what we love, or giving ourselves at the service of others. Maybe our greatest sacrifice will come with the physical or spiritual suffering of a loved one, or our own physical pain; by defeat in a race, occupation, or enterprise; or by witnessing the separation of our loved ones from God and from His Church. Sorrow and sacrifice have many nuances, as unique and beautiful as the person who carries them in his body or soul. The worth and beauty of the cross is *exalted* by the measure in which sacrifice is offered out of love and with love, united to *Jesus'* Cross. Its value *increases* by the measure in which we allow God to guide and instruct us about the type of sacrifices that we must offer (to be agreeable to Him, and to help Him in the salvation of souls). Most of us—as Saint Therese of Lisieux taught us—are *not* called to do heroic acts to please the Lord. The Heart of Jesus is not only consoled by spectacular sacrifices; we can contribute to the salvation of souls doing the *small* things of our daily life with *great* love and *purity* of intention. "God bestows more consideration on the purity of intention with which our actions are performed, than to the actions themselves." [254]

According to Our Divine Master, "take care not to perform righteous deeds in order that people may see them; otherwise, you will have no recompense from your heavenly Father." [255] May God, *exclusively*, know our sacrifices. We must not grow weary. God knows and sees *everything!* The Most Blessed Trinity is always with us, accompanies us, and—in fact—gives us the graces and strength we need to be able to offer the sacrifices that He inspires within us. Let us generously embrace these graces and transform them into *works*. We must *not* fear *sacrifice* because it is a *great gift* from God, which draws us close to His Sacred Heart and makes us similar to Him. Father Pio of Pietrelcina and Urs von Balthasar said that "the angels only envy us for one thing: they cannot suffer for God." When we feel that we have suffered too much, let us look at Jesus Crucified, at Saint Josephine Bakhita, at Padre Pio (who lived with the bleeding wounds of Our Lord for more than fifty years!), or at any other saint who inspires us to generosity. Let us ask them to intercede for us before the Father so that He may send us the gift of His Spirit of strength and help us to fulfill His most Holy Will. Again, let us *not* grow weary: God will *never* ask us to suffer more than what we can bear! On the other hand, since the cross (our

---

254 Saint Augustine of Hippo. Father and Doctor of the Church.

255 Matthew 6:1

suffering) is our *way to Heaven*, if we do not seek it *actively*—in His immense love and Mercy— God will send it to us, and it will be perfectly shaped to our size!

C) Living in the truth. The person who seeks the truth finds God because God is *The* Truth. Whoever knows and loves God enjoys perfect joy and happiness. Saint Augustine might be the best example of this reality. In his confessions, he declared that the lack of truth caused him to fall very low: "Woe, woe, by what steps I was dragged down to 'the depths of hell' toiling and fuming because of my lack of truth." [256] Yet, even when in his youth he was very far away from God, Augustine's passion for this truth—which he did not possess, but which he searched for unceasingly—led him to become a great saint and a defender and Doctor of the Church. "Where I found Truth, there found I my God, who is the Truth. From the time I learned this I have not forgotten" [257].

If we want God's indescribable beauty to be evident in our life, we must earnestly seek the truth and be honest, sincere, and coherent. "If a kingdom is divided against itself, that kingdom cannot stand." [258] *Without sincerity and coherence,* we are divided, and thus, we lack the strength produced by integrity. We become weak, an easy prey for the temptations and difficulties of life and of the devil—which defeat us—leaving us submerged in discouragement and depression. "What can be more glorious than

---

[256] Confessions Book 3, chapter 6, No. 11.

[257] Confessions Book 10, chapter 24, No. 35.

[258] Mark 3:24

being defeated by *The Truth*?" [259] Let us allow God to conquer us! His Grace, Love, and Truth will lead us to the *true happiness* and to reflect the true beauty, which is found in the soul united to God.

D) *Practicing purity*. Socrates [260] taught that "the truth cannot be seen with bodily eyes, but with a *purified* mind, and every soul in its possession becomes happy and perfect." The Greek philosopher did not know the True God, but if we recall Jesus' words "Blessed are the pure in heart, for they shall see God," [261] we can understand that Socrates' reasoning is perfectly valid. "Chastity or cleanness of heart holds a glorious and distinguished place among the virtues, because she, alone, enables man to see God." [262] We can only imitate what we see. If we wish to "see" God (to know Him deeply so we can imitate Him) we must try to live a life of purity, modesty, and fidelity. "The lamp of the body is the eye. If your eye is sound, your whole body will be filled with light." [263]

> *A pure soul is like a fine pearl. As long as it is hidden in the shell at the bottom of the sea, no one thinks of admiring it. But if you bring it into the sunshine, this pearl will shine and attract all eyes. Thus, the pure soul, which is hidden from the eyes*

---

[259] Saint Augustine of Hippo. Father and Doctor of the Church. *Expositions on the Book of Psalms*, pages 57,20.

[260] Greek Philosopher (470 BC – 399 BC).

[261] Matthew 5:8.

[262] Saint Augustine of Hippo, Father and Doctor of the Church.

[263] Matthew 6:22.

> *of the world, will one day shine before the Angels in the sunshine of eternity.* [264]

Would you like to have a radiant beauty? The answer is distant from a perfect make-up! It resides in a *pure soul*, because the *true dazzling beauty*, far from being external, comes from within!

E) Living lovingly. That we may be loving in our relationships with others is God's desire but also an *order!* "I give you a new *commandment:* love one another, as I have loved you." [265] Jesus' commandment is TO LOVE AS *HE* HAS LOVED US. He left the Father and came into the world to give us a clear and living example of what *true* love is. Jesus taught us that love is generous and detached from everything—for love of God and neighbor, and to "seek what is above" [266]. Most especially, Jesus taught us that love is total, unreserved, and willing to undergo the most extreme sacrifices for the beloved. If we have not grasped yet "what is the breadth, and length, and height and depth" [267] of God's love for each one of us, let us beg Him for this grace. Everyone—without exception—is deeply loved by the Lord, who is "Goodness and Beauty, beginning, cause, and source of everything that is good and lovely." [268] God is *constantly* seeking for you and me. Let us not

[264] St. John Marie Vianney (Holy Cure of Ars).

[265] John 13:34

[266] Colossians 3:1

[267] Ephesians 3:17-20

[268] Saint Augustine of Hippo. Soliloquies - Book I, Chapter I, *Prayer to God.* No. 3.

hide anymore; let us go out to His encounter and trustfully throw ourselves into His arms. "I have always seen in my God, way bigger and exalted proofs of love, than the ones I ever desired or asked for" [269] He is faithful, He will *never* leave us, and His love for us will *never* cease. "…and, since God has first loved us, love is now no longer a mere 'command', it is the response to the gift of love with which God draws near to us." [270] Let us try to respond to Love, acting lovingly, sharing God's love—which we have received so freely and so generously—with everyone; and let us *not* allow ourselves, nor allow anyone else, to separate us from this beautiful love.

> *God, to be separated from you is to fall; to come to you is to be raised; to remain in you is to be firm. God, turning our backs on you is to die. To be converted to You is to live again, to dwell in You is to live. God, whom nobody can lose, unless deceived; whom nobody searches, unless warned; whom nobody finds, except when purified. God, leaving You is to die; following You is to love …* [271]

God is Love, Goodness, Perfection, and Beauty in its utmost splendor. Only the person who *loves* can be beautiful because he becomes a *reflection* of God. Indeed, the exterior beauty that we see in a person is only a reflection of God's Beauty—found

[269] Saint Teresa of Avila, Doctor of the Church.

[270] His Holiness Benedict XVI – Encyclical Letter "Deus Caritas Est", No. 1.

[271] Saint Augustine of Hippo. Soliloquies - Book I, Chapter I *Prayer to God.* No. 3.

within every heart—and it is manifested outwardly in the measure in which the Lord takes possession of his being … The person in whom God has made His dwelling place possesses an *exceptional beauty*. "Only if I *serve* my neighbor can my eyes be opened to what God does for me and how much He loves me." [272] Whoever tries to resemble God in His love for others (manifested through unselfish service, compassion, tenderness, and a disposition to help *everyone* in their problems, needs, and difficulties) will become a reflection of The Blessed Trinity—of His Beauty and Kindness. "Your heavenly Father makes His sun rise on the evil and on the good, and sends rain on the just and on the unjust." [273] Even when in the eyes of the world it may seem madness—just as Jesus' Cross seemed "folly to Gentiles" [274]—loving and doing good to everyone (friends and enemies alike) bring us close to the Lord, help us to resemble God's Heart, and fill us with the experience of His love … and the person who *knows* he is loved, becomes "*joyfully radiant*"*!* "'Let the hearts of those who seek the LORD rejoice.' Although man can forget God or reject Him, He never ceases to call every man to seek Him, so as to find life and happiness…"[275] *True happiness* is found when we sincerely seek God. This sincere search can be achieved through:

- interior life (prayer and silence)
- joyful sacrifice
- passion for the truth

---

272 H.H. Benedict XVI – Encyclical Letter "Deus Caritas Est", No. 18.

273 Matthew 5:45

274 1 Corinthians 1:23

275 Catechism of the Catholic Church-No. 30.

- purity (which opens our eyes to His presence)
- and by loving others (this helps us understand the greatness of Divine love for us).

Once we have found the Lord, let us ask Him for the graces of perseverance, fidelity, and humility, so that—emptied of ourselves—He may live and reign within our hearts. The Blessed Virgin Mary is the best and highest expression of this reality because, "She who belongs to the 'humble and poor of the Lord' bears in Herself, like no other member of the human race, that ' glory of grace' which the Father 'has bestowed on us in his beloved Son,' and this *grace determines the extraordinary greatness and beauty* of Her whole being." [276] Any person who truly knows Mary, is able to recognize Her unparalleled physical and spiritual beauty. "All my own perception of beauty, both in majesty and simplicity, is founded upon Our Lady."[277] In the excess of Your generosity and Mercy, give us, O Lord, that *exceptional beauty*—which indicates that you have taken possession of our souls—like you did in the soul of Mary! Amen.

[276] Pope St. John Paul II, Encyclical Letter *Redemptoris Mater* - No. 11.

[277] J.R.R Tolkien. Writer and English Poet (1892-1973).

CHAPTER XII: The Woman of Contradictions

Mother… I can't find a better expression to describe Her. The best, most tender, the sweetest and purest among all women; nonetheless, the strongest and most powerful intercessor and advocate before Almighty God. There are no words to manifest Her greatness. She is the Queen of Heaven and Earth and—in contrast—the humblest, simplest, and the poorest among all creatures. The heart exults and —at the same time—it is filled with peace by the mere sound of Her name: *Mary!* "Mary is more excellent than all, by nature fair and beautiful, and more holy than the Cherubim and Seraphim. To praise Her all the tongues of Heaven and earth *do not* suffice"[278].

"Mary is the image and model of all mothers, of their great mission to be guardians of life, of their mission to be teachers in the art of living and loving." [279] The soul who embraces the Blessed Virgin's motherly care will receive Her tenderness and exquisite care; this blessed soul will learn to *live* and to *give life*; Our Lady will teach him to love, to be a better person, a better father, and a better Christian. "Mary seeks for those who approach Her devoutly and with reverence, for such She loves, nourishes, and adopts as Her children" [280].

278 Pope Pius IX. Apostolic Constitution *Ineffabilis Deus*. On the Immaculate Conception. December 8, 1854.

279 His Holiness Benedict XVI – Valencia (Spain) – V World encounter with the families-City of Arts and Sciences- Sunday, July 9, 2006.

280 Saint Bonaventure–Doctor of the Church (1221-1274)

Sadly, many of us fallen creatures often have hardened hearts, "hearts of stone." [281] Maybe, this is the reason for which we cannot totally comprehend and accept the extraordinary gift that *God* has bestowed upon us when—from the Cross—*He* gave us *Mary* as our Mother.[282] Could our hardened hearts be the reason for which—at times—we fear approaching the Blessed Virgin, thus falling in the *snare* of thinking that She is going to "take" the place that belongs to God only? The Venerable Fulton J. Sheen reminded us, "Let those who think that the Church pays too much attention to Mary, give heed to the fact that Our Blessed Lord Himself, gave ten times as much of His life to Her, as He gave to His Apostles." And Saint Maximilian Kolbe said, "If anyone does not wish to have Mary Immaculate for his Mother, he will not have Christ for His Brother". Do we forget that children love their mothers, and mothers love their children, and that their only desire is the well-being of each one of them? Without a doubt, a mother always desires that her children may be known, loved, and accepted! The reason for which Christ is unknown today is because His Mother is unknown—and even worse: She is insulted, despised, and rejected—by many! Let us know and love the Blessed Virgin Mary with filial tenderness and without fear. Let us offer reparation to Her Immaculate Heart for all the offenses She receives. She helps us to know, love, and welcome Her Son Jesus in our hearts and in our lives. Who can ever know the son better than the mother (who carried him in her womb, gave birth to him, and saw him grow)?

---

[281] Ezekiel 36:26

[282] John 19:27

"'Show us Jesus.' Show to us pilgrims the one who is both the way and the destination: the Truth and the Life." [283]

Saint Louis De Montfort, in his book *True Devotion to the Blessed Virgin Mary*, expressed in a simple—but extremely wise manner—the importance of loving and embracing Mary with a sincere heart. He reminded us about the Divine immutability and wisdom:

> *The Most High God came down to us in a perfect way through the humble Virgin Mary without losing anything of his divinity or holiness. It is likewise through Mary that we, poor creatures, must ascend to almighty God in a perfect manner without having anything to fear.* [284]

Jesus came into this world through Mary, and since God does not change—in His infinite Wisdom—He is still choosing the same way to come to us, and for us to go to Him: *Mary*.

> *For just as this star [the morning star], together with the 'dawn,' precedes the rising of the sun, so Mary—from the time of Her Immaculate Conception—preceded the coming of the Savior,*

[283] His Holiness Benedict XVI – Homily during the Mass in the Sanctuary of Mariazell – September 8, 2007.

[284] *Preparation for the Total Consecration*. Saint Louis Marie De Montfort. 3rd Part, day 24.

> *the rising of the 'Sun of Justice' in the history of the human race.* [285]

Whomever loves Mary can have full *certitude* of finding and loving *Jesus!*

We are all Mary's children, but only those who keep very close to Her—exclusively those who *open their heart* to Her maternal teachings—can obtain the graces needed to live in justice and righteousness, with purity and fidelity to God.

> *The greatest saints—those richest in grace and virtue—will be the most assiduous in praying to the most Blessed Virgin, looking up to Her as the perfect model to imitate, and as a powerful helper to assist them.* [286]

Because of all Her virtues "Her profound humility, Her lively faith, Her blind obedience, Her continual mental prayer, Her mortification in all things, Her surpassing purity, Her ardent charity, Her heroic patience, Her angelic sweetness and Her divine wisdom," [287] Mary is the *elected vessel*—pure, sacred and intact—chosen by God, so that we may ascend to Him. Her Motherly Heart is full of tenderness; Her power of intercession obtains unimaginable graces for all Her children. "Only after the Last Judgment will Mary get any rest; from now until then, She is much

---

[285] Pope Saint John Paul II, Encyclical letter *Redemptoris Mater* Introduction, No. 3.

[286] Saint Louis Marie De Montfort.

[287] Saint Louis Marie De Montfort. *True Devotion to the Blessed Virgin Mary.*

too busy with Her children." [288] The ever-Blessed Virgin Mary generously, unconditionally, and unceasingly intercedes—with true motherly love—for *all* Her children (for those who know Her, love Her, want Her, and for those who *do not*) because a true mother makes *no* differences; she loves all her children equally and offers up her work, prayers, and her entire life for each and every one of them. "Let us run to Mary, and, as Her little children, cast ourselves into Her arms with perfect confidence" [289] because She will *never* disappoint us!

From the beginning of Christianity, Mary's power of intercession has been recognized:

> *The foundation of all our confidence rests in the Blessed Virgin Mary. God has committed to Her the treasury of all good things, in order that everyone may know that through Her are obtained every hope, every grace, and all salvation. For this is His Will: That we obtain everything through Mary.* [290]

The Lord—who is infinitely generous—wishes to fill us with every good thing through the intercessory prayers of the Blessed Virgin Mary; She is Jesus's sweet Mother, but also "the handmaid of the Lord." The Blessed Virgin Mary pleases God *always* by fulfilling His Most Holy Will and by interceding for us with the purest heart—which is also the most humble and full of

---

288 Saint John Marie Vianney [The holy Cure of Ars (1786–1859)].

289 Saint Francis de Sales, Doctor of the Church (1567-1622).

290 Pope Pius IX. Encyclical Letter *Ubi Primum*. February 2nd, 1849.

love and respect for Her Creator, that ever existed. *Nobody* prays like Mary! Our Heavenly Mother rejoices when we share with Her the experience of God's presence in our soul. She is deeply happy when we understand God's Beauty and infinite generosity through contemplation. She rejoices when Her children enjoy the Lord's sweetness and magnanimity, and when they obtain His favors. Through Jesus' first miracle, we understand Mary's great power of intercession: "With your prayer at Cana in Galilee, you achieved that the Heart of Jesus were revealed in its generosity." [291] Because of the Blessed Virgin Mary's intercession, Jesus bestowed His first miracle; throughout the centuries uncountable graces and miracles have been granted, thanks to His Mother's most powerful and humble prayers for us. "If anyone invokes the Mother of God and takes Her as Patroness in the important matters, the only thing that can happen is that *everything* will go *well* and that it will result in the *glory* of the good Jesus, Her Son." [292]

A little child always finds security in the loving gaze of his mother. "In trials or difficulties, I resort to Mother Mary, whose gaze is enough to dissipate any fear" [293]. There are some people for whom "spiritual infancy" is difficult to understand, and that is fine. Nevertheless, in His preaching, Jesus said, "I thank you, Father, Lord of Heaven and earth, that You have *hidden* these things from the wise and understanding and *revealed* them to infants." [294] And the Word Incarnate—*Almighty God*—became a Little Child, a tiny babe in the arms of Mary. Whoever decides to become a "little

---

[291] Pope St. John Paul II – Angelus, Sunday, August 3, 1986.

[292] Saint Vincent de Paul CXIV, 126.

[293] Saint Thérèse of Lisieux. Doctor of the Church (1873-1897).

[294] Matthew 11:25

child" in Mary's arms will always be safe. He will find the answers to his questions and difficulties without too much toil, because his Mother—having him in the fold of Her arms—will help him.

> *Let nothing disturb your heart or your countenance. Am I not here, who am your Mother? Are you not under my shadow and protection? Are you not in the folds of my mantle? In the crossing of my arms? Is there anything else you need?* [295]

These are *the Mother's* words—who in diverse occasions—has descended to us to give us Her love and consolation, to guide and protect us, and to warn us of the dangers of the world and of sin. She knows that we live in a "valley of tears" and understands that we need someone to wipe those tears away. "If you ever feel distressed during your day call upon Our Lady. Just say this simple prayer: 'Mary, Mother of Jesus, please be a mother to me now.' I must admit that this prayer has never failed me." [296] Our Lady has appeared on different occasions and with different names: Our Lady of Guadalupe, Our Lady of Fatima, Our Lady of Akita, Our Lady of Lourdes, Our Lady of the Volcans (Lanzarote), Our Lady of la Salette, Our Lady of Knock, etc.; but there is only one Mary: The Mother of God and our Mother. Let us listen to Her—and aided by Her—let us change our sinful life into a peaceful, just, truthful, and loving life!

---

295 Words of the Blessed Virgin Mary to Saint Juan Diego (1531).

296 Saint Mother Teresa of Calcutta.

By God's design—because of Her humility, simplicity, and sweetness—Mary has been placed as our *best* defense against the attacks of the enemy of our souls. [297] Therefore, the best protection against his snares, and against any danger, is to promptly ask for our Mother's help. "If you invoke the Blessed Virgin when you are tempted, She will come at once to your help, and satan will leave you." [298] There have been numerous movies in which one of the superheroes has the power to create indestructible "force camps." We can say that the Blessed Virgin Mary is something like that—though much more superior: Her protection is so powerful, so strong, and so great, that not even the sharpest—or the most piercing—arms of the enemy of our souls, can penetrate or harm us if *She* is our defense. "Men do not fear a powerful hostile army as the powers of hell *fear* the name and protection of *Mary*." [299] Whoever lives under Mary's protection has *nothing* to fear!

> *Let the storm rage and the sky darken—not for that shall we be dismayed ... If we trust as we should in Mary ... we shall recognize in Her, that Virgin Most Powerful 'who with virginal foot did crush the head of the serpent.'* [300]

Let us ask Mary to obtain for us the grace of conquering sin and evil in our life and in the life of those we love. Let us ask Her to

---

[297] Genesis 3:15.

[298] Saint John Marie Vianney (The Holy Cure of Ars).

[299] Saint Bonaventure.

[300] Pope Pius X. Encyclical letter *Ad Diem Illum Laetissimum* (On the Inmaculate Conception). February 2nd, 1904. No. 33.

help us live like Her: serving the Lord and our neighbor with love and humility, with generosity and sincere surrender, and always in profound friendship with God. If we obtain this grace, we will be able to live "happily ever after" with Her and the most Blessed Trinity, in Heaven.

Because God so willed it (as He did with Adam and Eve), the Blessed Virgin Mary was created *without* the stain of original sin. This special grace of having been born without sin did not exempt Her from experiencing temptation—just as the Creator did not free from temptation Adam, Eve, and not even Jesus Himself[301] (because He was true God, but also, true man). In spite of that, the Blessed Virgin Mary—as Her Beloved Son—remained *always* faithful to the Father and preserved that state of virginal purity and sinlessness in Her body, mind, and soul *every day* of Her life.

Throughout our life, God gifts us with marvelous people: true examples of love of Him and neighbor—who deserve to be admired and imitated ... Why not turn our gaze to the *worthiest* of all praise, the "Queen of all Saints," and allow ourselves to be captivated by the admirable beauty of Her soul? Mary is "more beautiful than beauty, more gracious than grace." [302] During Her life on Earth, Our Lady had *unlimited* love, purity, and fidelity; She *lovingly* and *selflessly* accepted the Lord's Will, and kept *unswerving* faith and hope in God—even amidst the deepest sorrows and confusion.[303] Mary truly was the "handmaid of the Lord" and by humbly saying "yes," She became the Mother of the

---

[301] Matthew 4:1-11.

[302] S.S. Pius IX. Apostolic Constitution *Ineffabilis Deus*. December 8th, 1854.

[303] Annunciation (Luke 1:26-38); Passion and death of Her Son Jesus Christ (John 18:19).

Only Begotten Son of the Father—bringing us salvation. Without a doubt, the Blessed Virgin Mary *deserves to be loved, venerated, admired, and imitated!*

Mary "stands out among the poor and humble of the Lord, who confidently hope for, and receive salvation from Him." [304] Given our sinful condition, which makes us offend the Lord again and again [305], we are *truly unworthy* of approaching God's altar and the Lord Himself—who has been and always is so infinitely Good to us. Fortunately, Jesus has given us His Holy Mother so that She may be our Mother too and our intercessor before Him. "Regardless of how bad our sins have been, if we are devoted to Mary, it is impossible for us to be lost" [306] because "Mary provides the sinner with refuge and strength." [307] In the most difficult moments, when it is hard to discern which path to take when it is difficult to think clearly—and to make good decisions—let us come to Mary as our Guide, because She is the "Throne of Wisdom," the "Mother of Good Counsel," and the "Queen of Peace." Let us offer a sincere prayer to Our Mother, take Her by Her loving hand, and allow Her to shower us with the dew of Her tenderness and care. When we draw close to Mary and acknowledge that we are loved and cared by Her, our soul *flourishes* in God's sight. Our Lady leads us step by step—without rushing and with certitude— through the *safest path* to Her beloved Son. "As mariners are guided into port by the shining of a star, so

---

[304] *Lumen Gentium*, 55.

[305] Romans 7:19: "For I do not do the Good I want, but the evil I do not want is what I do."

[306] Saint Hillary of Poitiers.

[307] Saint Anthony of Padua.

Christians are guided to Heaven by Mary." [308] Whoever follows Mary in sincere love and in the imitation of Her virtues, *consoles* the Heart of Jesus and obtains eternal salvation. "Always remain close to this Celestial Mother, because She is the sea that must be crossed to reach the shores of Eternal Splendor" [309].

We cannot finish this chapter without mentioning the prayer of the Holy Rosary. Our Lady has many words of love and wisdom to share with us, but we will only hear Her if we pray the Rosary. When Mary appeared in Fatima, only two of the little visionaries could hear her. Francisco, who didn't particularly like this prayer, needed "to pray many Rosaries" before he could also hear the Queen of Heaven! If each and every Christian took the Rosary in our hands and prayed it *fervently* (at least once a day), the devil would be cast into hell, having *nothing* else to do on earth. Saint Pio of Pietrelcina called the Holy Rosary "the weapon." If we all prayed the Rosary *daily*, we would live in peace, harmony, unity, and purity because the Blessed Virgin Mary would obtain for us—as She *always* does—the grace of Divine protection and a true love for God and for others. "The Rosary … especially in the passage of difficult times, has ever [been] used for the accomplishment of *all* desires." [310] Pray the Rosary every day, my friend. The prayer of the Holy Rosary brings *fruits of eternity* into our souls: a "wonderful confirmation of faith, protection against the disease of error, and increase of the strength of the soul." [311] The prayer of the Holy Rosary has also won great battles, beginning

[308] Saint Thomas Aquinas.

[309] Saint Padre Pio of Pietrelcina.

[310] Pope Leo XIII. Encyclical on the Rosary *Octobri Mense*. September 22nd,1891

[311] Ibis. No. 7

with the Battle of Muret in 1213, and continuing with innumerable victories, like the Battle of Lepanto in 1571; the Battle of King Louis XIII in la Rochelle, France in 1627; the Battle of La Naval in Manila, the Philippines, in 1646 … More recently, during the bombardment of Hiroshima in 1945, eight Jesuit priests—who lived only a few blocks from the center of the explosion—miraculously survived amid an ocean of destruction which surrounded them. The miracle did not stop in the fact that they were unharmed by the bombardment. After many years, none of them suffered or died because of the radiation. Each one of them affirmed that this miracle had been granted to them because they lived in the "spirit of Fatima." In Fatima, the Blessed Virgin asked for *five first Saturdays* in reparation of Her Immaculate Heart, *sacrifice,* and for the *daily* recitation of the holy Rosary—and they had been faithful to Her calling. In this apparition, the Blessed Virgin also encouraged our trust and hope. She offered that we will be *victorious* in our daily struggles and in the battles that we must fight against a hostile world, because—She clearly said, "In the end, my Immaculate Heart will triumph." Let us live in constant union with the Queen of the Universe because She will teach us how to reach eternal life. Let us not fear serving in Her army because "To serve the Queen of Heaven is already to reign on this Earth, and to live under Her commands is more than to govern" [312].

Pope Saint John Paul II was well known for his great love of the Blessed Virgin Mary, and he wrote a prayer that we can repeat frequently:

---

[312] Saint John Marie Vianney.

> *Immaculate Conception, Mary my Mother: live in me, act in me, speak in and through me, think your thoughts in my mind, love through my heart. Give me your dispositions and feelings; teach, lead, and guide me to Jesus. Correct, enlighten, and expand my thoughts and behavior. Possess my soul; take over my entire personality and life and replace them with yourself. Incline me to constant adoration and thanksgiving. Pray in me and through me. Let me live in you and keep me in this union always. Amen*

Let us *not* reject Mary! She is *the best*, the most tender and caring of *all* mothers. Let us *seek* Her, *love* Her, and *welcome* Her frequently and as a true Mother. How happy we will be if we allow Her to cover us under Her soft, but safe mantle; if we permit Her to fill us with the beautiful scent of Her love, and to guide us— in the fold of Her arms—to the encounter with Jesus! She will obtain for us the joy of the *true happiness*, because "we never give more honor to Jesus than when we honor His Mother, and we honor Her simply and solely to honor *Him* all the more perfectly. We go to Her only as a *way* leading to the goal we seek—*Jesus*, Her Son" [313].

In this confidence, let us consecrate ourselves to Jesus through Mary. According to St. Louis De Montfort,

> *This devotion faithfully practiced produces countless happy effects in the soul. The most*

---

[313] Saint Louis De Montfort.

> *important of them is that it establishes—even here on earth—Mary's life in the soul, so that it is no longer the soul that lives, but Mary who lives in it. In a manner of speaking, Mary's soul becomes identified with the soul of Her servant. Indeed, when by an unspeakable but real grace Mary most holy becomes Queen of a soul, She works untold wonders in it. She is a great wonder-worker especially in the interior of souls ...* [314]

Let us thank the most Blessed Trinity for the wonderful gift of a spiritual Mother who *always* loves us, accompanies us, protects us, and cares for us. Let us turn our gaze to Mary *daily* and ask Her for the grace to live as Her *true* children until Her Immaculate Heart brings to completion the kingship of Jesus—Her Son—in our soul.

> *We are firm in our confidence that She ... will obtain pardon for the sinner, health for the sick, strength of heart for the weak, consolation for the afflicted, help for those in danger; that She will remove spiritual blindness from all who are in error, so that they may return to the path of truth and justice, and that there may be one flock under one shepherd.* [315]

---

314 St. Louis de Montfort, *The Secret of Mary,* No. 55.

315 S.S. Pius IX. Apostolic Constitution *Ineffabilis Deus*. December 8th, 1854.

CONCLUSION

True happiness exists and its name is *GOD:* Father, Son, and Holy Ghost. He is our *ultimate end* and our *noblest* and *truest goal.* Jesus Christ is the Way, the Truth, and the Life [316] of every man and woman. In our lives there are ups and downs, moments of joy and sorrow, smiles and tears. If we remain faithful to Him—especially in the difficult moments (in the moments of confusion, sorrow, pain, and tragedy)—*without complaining, but humbly accepting His Will*—which is *always* wise, holy, and loving—LIFE IS BEAUTIFUL AND WORTH LIVING.

God grants us this life "to know Him, love Him, serve Him, and to be happy with Him for all eternity." He is always with us because God is *faithful.* And to help us walk this path, He gives us His grace, offers His help, and teaches us that we must "conquer evil with good" [317] and hatred with love. How? By living diligently, fervently, joyfully, and with a heart full of hope; by following Jesus' footsteps: being patient in tribulation, persevering in prayer, looking for opportunities to be hospitable, blessing those who persecute us, rejoicing with those who rejoice, mourning with those who mourn, living in humility, returning good for evil, trying to be at peace with everyone, and helping our enemies. [318] "Our desires for well-being and happiness will be satisfied only and truly, when peoples, families and when the whole society lives according to the commandment of love … Humanity … cannot find its own

316 John 14:6

317 Romans 12:21

318 Romans 12:11-21.

fulfillment but only when it surrenders itself, sincerely to others."[319] Let us adhere to God, who is the true source of love and of every good thing. "Peace is the outcome of a long and demanding battle which is *only* won when evil is defeated *by good* … At its deepest level, evil is a *tragic rejection* of the demands of love." [320] Let us *freely* choose goodness and love with *all* their *demands*. Let us *never* get discouraged when facing this long and hard battle because

> *The perfection we desire to attain is not acquired once and for all; perfection means journeying on. It is continuous readiness to move ahead because we never attain a perfect likeness to God; we are always on our way. The history of every soul is that of a love which fills every time and at the same time is open to new horizons, for God continually stretches the soul's possibilities to make it capable of ever greater goods. God himself, who has sown the seeds of good in us and from whom every initiative of holiness stems, 'models the block ... and polishing and cleansing our spirit, forms Christ within us.'* [321]

Let us live with purity, humility, and charity, the "keys" which open the doors of Heaven and of men's hearts. Let us seek

---

[319] Pope St. John Paul II – Willemstad (Netherland Antilles) Sunday, May 13, 1990. No. 3.

[320] Pope St. John Paul II – World Day of Peace – January 1st, 2005.

[321] H.H Benedict XVI – General Audience – September 5, 2007.

sacrifice and truth. Like Saint Augustine, "you are called to be a passionate seeker of the truth, of high and noble ideals. Do *not* fall in the trap of apathy, indifference, nor despair. The Lord is with you. Be, therefore, a protagonist in the construction of a more just, a healthier and more fraternal society." [322] It is in our hands to do this, but in order to accomplish it, we must be "new creatures."

The following words are from Pope Saint John Paul II to the youth, and a perfect summary of this book:

> *What Jesus does promise is that His victory over sin and death can also be your victory, if—in imitation of His Cross—you consent to 'lose your life' together with Him, that is, to offer your life to the Father; to spend your life in love for others, even strangers, enemies, and those who sin against you; to seek God's will and not your own in all things. This is what it means to be a new creation: to share in divine life, to be freed from sin and restored to the likeness of God, so that here and now you may build His kingdom of peace, justice, and love, and one day share eternal happiness with Him in Heaven.* [323]

This book is just a small "appetizer." We must feast now on the splendid banquet found in the Sacred Scripture (especially in

---

[322] Homily of Pope Saint John Paul II in Willemstad (Dutch Antilles) Sunday, May 13th, 1990. No. 6.

[323] Ibid.

the Gospels) and in the books which contain the wisdom of the Fathers of the Church and of the saints. This will help us to continue to grow in our love for the Lord, for His Church, and for His souls.

True happiness exists and its name is God. May *He* help and bless—with His grace—the *good resolutions* that have sprung up in our soul while reading this little book. May the Lord also bless our *sincere efforts* to achieve these goals. May the Most Blessed Trinity live in your soul so that everyone who sees you may exclaim, "this man has found the *true happiness!*" Lord, make our hearts burn in Your love so that we may be able to transmit that fire to others! Amen.

APPENDIX

“Oh my God, I believe, I adore, I hope and I love You, and I beg pardon for those who do not believe, do not adore, do not hope and do not love Thee. O Most Blessed Trinity, I adore Thee profoundly. My God, my God, how much I love Thee in the Most Blessed Sacrament.”

–Prayer of Portugal’s Angel

“O Most Holy Trinity, Father, Son and Holy Ghost, I adore Thee profoundly. I offer Thee the most precious Body, Blood, Soul and Divinity of Jesus Christ present in all the tabernacles of the world, in reparation for the outrages, sacrileges and indifferences by which He is offended. Through the infinite merits of His most Sacred Heart and of the Immaculate Heart of Mary, I beg of You the conversion of poor sinners.”

–Prayer of Portugal’s Angel

“May the most holy, most sacred, most adorable, most incomprehensible, and ineffable Name of God be forever praised, blessed, adored, loved, and glorified, in heaven, on earth, and under the earth, by all the creatures of God, and by the Sacred Heart of Our Lord Jesus Christ in the most Holy Sacrament of the Altar. Amen.”

–The Golden Arrow Prayer

“I love You, O my God, and my only desire is to love you until the last breath of my life. I love You, O my infinitely lovable God, and I would rather die loving You, than live without loving You. I love You, Lord and the only grace I ask is to love You eternally. My God, if my tongue cannot say in every moment that I love You, I want my heart to repeat it to You as often as I draw breath. Amen.”

–Saint John Marie Vianney

"Take, Lord, and receive all my liberty, my memory, my understanding, and my entire will. All I have and call my own. You have given all to me. To you, Lord, I return it. Everything is yours; do with it what you will. Give me only your love and your grace, that is enough for me. Amen."

–Saint Ignatius of Loyola

"Teach us, good Lord, to serve you as you deserve, to give and not to count the cost, to fight and not to heed the wounds, to toil and not to seek for rest, to labor and not to ask for any reward, save that of knowing that we do your will. Amen."

–Saint Ignatius of Loyola

"Mary, my dearest Mother, give me your heart so beautiful, so pure, so immaculate, your heart so full of love and humility, that I may be able to receive Jesus in the Bread of Life, love Him as you loved Him and serve Him in the distressing disguise of the poorest of the poor."

–Saint Mother Teresa of Calcutta

"At last I love Thee alone, Thee alone follow, Thee alone seek, Thee alone am I ready to serve: for Thou alone, by right, art ruler; under Thy rule do I wish to be. Command, I pray, and order what Thou wilt, but heal and open my ears that I may hear Thy commands, heal and open my eyes, that I may see Thy nod; cast all unsoundness from me that I may recognize Thee! Tell me whither to direct my gaze, that I may look upon Thee, and I hope that I shall do all things which Thou commandest! … I feel that I ought to return to Thee: let Thy door open to me knocking: teach me, Thou, how to come to Thee … do Thou suggest it, make it plain, equip me for the journey! "

–Saint Augustine of Hippo

"Come, divine Spirit, send forth the heavenly radiance of your light. Loving father of the poor. Gift, splendid giver of gifts; Light which penetrates our souls. Source of our greatest consolation.

Come, sweet guest of the soul. In labor, you are our rest; in hard labor, truce; in heat, breeze; in tears, joy; in grief, comfort. Fill the inmost souls of your faithful, O most blessed light, and enrich us. See the emptiness of men, when you are not within us; see the power of sin, when you don't breathe on us; water the parched land; heal the wounded heart. Wash what is spotted; infuse fire in that which is chilled; tame the wild; lead what goes astray. Give to your faithful, those who trust in you, the sevenfold gifts. Through your kindness and grace, grant merits to our efforts; save those who seek salvation, and grant us eternal joy. Amen."

–Prayer to the Holy Ghost

Corporal Works of Mercy: To feed the hungry; to give water to the thirsty; to clothe the naked; to shelter the homeless; to visit the sick; to visit the imprisoned, or ransom the captive; to bury the dead.

Spiritual Works of Mercy: To instruct the ignorant; to counsel the doubtful; to admonish the sinners; to bear patiently those who wrong us; to forgive offenses; to comfort the afflicted; to pray for the living and the dead.

P.R.C.A.G.D.

Made in the USA
Las Vegas, NV
24 March 2025

20074698R00098